LUTHER BURBANK

ALFRED BURRANY   FREDERICK W. CLAMPETT.

LUTHER BURBANK
"OUR BELOVED INFIDEL"

His Religion of Humanity

BY

FREDERICK W. CLAMPETT

GREENWOOD PRESS, PUBLISHERS
WESTPORT, CONNECTICUT

Originally published in 1926
by The Macmillan Company, New York

First Greenwood Reprinting 1970

Library of Congress Catalogue Card Number 73-109720

SBN 8371-4210-5

Printed in the United States of America

To
My Wife

INTRODUCTORY NOTE

Luther Burbank has certainly earned a right to speak to the world, in the name of religion as well as in that of science.

He has long been a national figure and, in scientific circles, a world figure.

As a life-long student of science, and as an independent thinker, it was natural that an appeal should be made to him for his views on the relation of science to religion. His experience has led him far away from much that now claims as its own the name of Christianity, but which in his mind has absorbed much which bears no relation to the teachings of Jesus. At the same time he cannot conceive that constantly increasing knowledge of the physical universe stands in opposition to "pure religion," as shown in lives made beautiful and sweet by self-devotion and self-restraint and undefiled by subservience to superstition and man-made authority.

The only religion which endures must be hand in hand with that science which also endures.

Luther Burbank was the most noted of all the many men engaged, the world over, in plant breeding.

In the finest of all arts, the production of useful and beautiful plants through crossing, selection and segregation, his work rests on the teachings of Charles Darwin, tested and verified in the sixty-seven years

7

since the publication of *The Origin of Species* by thousands on thousands of naturalists, Darwin's colleagues and disciples.

The conception of organic evolution, or orderly change in the succession of living beings, demonstrated by Darwin though not originated by him, is now an unquestioned part of science, as much so as the theory of gravitation. All discussion of life problems, from the generation of amœbæ to the development of human society, must be related to it and more or less based upon it.

But while no one who has seriously studied the question of evolution from any angle has any doubts of the main principle, there is much divergence of opinion as to the relative value of the factors which have brought about the transmutation of species, and as to how this relatively new accession of knowledge may affect the religious feelings of humanity, and especially the organizations which have grown up around them. Every new expansion of knowledge has its effect on the time-honored sanctions upon which organizations rest or claim to rest.

The result of all observation and experiment is to show two great basal facts: first, that Nature in all its ramifications is in *process of change;* second, that *all change is orderly: nowhere is there disorder or chaos.* Thus everywhere and at all times in the universe, so far as we know, *orderly change is present.* Nature is, therefore, inseparable from it. Thus Vernon Kellogg has asserted: "Nature and Evolution are one and the same thing." As we believe that a cause stands before every effect, our highest duty in Nature is to find out, so far as we can, how her changes are brought about, then to search out, as well as we can, the nature and source of the rational order which pervades all phenomena. For in the universe, as Huxley has phrased it, "Nothing endures save the flow of energy and the *rational* order which pervades it."

That a rational basis of order exists, few men have ever questioned. That this is a beneficent personal intelligence is widely, even generally accepted, even by those who regard it as unknowable as well as infinite. For with our limitations we are obliged to use human phraseology, even when we realize that it must diverge infinitely from the infinite truth itself. Perhaps no man can wholly escape from some phase of anthropomorphism. For to the measure of a man, all that any man can conceive must in some degree be brought.

The present volume has been prepared as a summary of Luther Burbank's experiences and beliefs. His interpreter here is Dr. Frederick W. Clampett, a friend at once broad-minded and sympathetic. Dr. Clampett has been for over forty years a clergyman in the Protestant Episcopal Church, and has been long honored as one of its wise and liberal representatives.

During the World War he served as Chaplain of the 144th Field Artillery (the "Grizzlies") in France, having received his commission direct from the hands of the late President Wilson.

He has been a writer on world topics for the past five years, three of which have been spent in Europe.

DAVID STARR JORDAN
Chancellor, Stanford University

CONTENTS

Contents

LUTHER BURBANK

AN APPRECIATION

Luther Burbank is perhaps the most widely known and least understood of modern scientists. This failure to understand him aright is due to the publication of many detached fragments of his life which have been lacking in logical sequence and true proportion. And those detached fragments confine themselves almost exclusively to the scientific aspects of his long and remarkable career.

To know Luther Burbank as he was, from the human, the scientific and the spiritual sides of his nature is to become acquainted with one of the most fascinating personalities of our times. It is to receive a demonstration that his triumph in the realm of science is more than equaled by his triumph in the realm of spirit.

His religious experiences and beliefs, as told in these subsequent pages, will be more clearly understood in the setting provided by the events that helped to shape his career, and in the light cast by the slow, patient methods that marked his pursuit of clues in science.

My purpose in this preface will be to present in brief form those hitherto obscured aspects of his character and in that way strive to depict certain features of his life unknown to the public that give it sym-

metry. The best means to use in doing this is to
make a composite study of the man, which shall be
the outcome of twenty years of close personal friendship. It is a story, the world will say, of intense human
interest; and one of the highest inspiration, will be
the verdict of the seeker after truth.

His onward march along the tedious, oftentimes
painful, treks of the scientist blazed many a fresh
trail into "the infinite variety and unity of Nature."

Underneath it all, as a foundation that "standeth
sure," is the spiritual man, his "Kingdom within" in
tune with the Infinite.

These two aspects of his character help to explain
his feeling that the creeds enmeshed in superstition
and bigotry occupy the antipodes of the world in
which he dwelt himself, and that the silent growth of
his quite different beliefs was the product of his own
judgment and reason, based on the primal responses
of his being "to the voice within."

On its human side Luther Burbank's life, in its
play with science, presents a study bristling with
romance. Measured by the intenseness of the strain
and the ups and downs fortune played him in his
long-drawn-out struggle against heavy odds, no other
life in the realm of science contains more startling
antitheses.

This thought moved and mastered me as I stood
beside him on the lawn of his Santa Rosa home the
day of the fiftieth anniversary of his life-work in California.

Who could have believed, that radiant morning,
that this man frolicking on the grass with the light-

heartedness of a child was within close sight of his seventy-seventh milestone!

Of lithe, spare figure, below the average height, with mind and muscle striving for added proficiency, the spirit of youth kindling his eye, pure kindness reflected in his gentle, genial face, he looked as able as one of his favorite plants to serve as a living incarnation expressing the truth of selection, heredity and training.

Luther Burbank in his "seventies" was psychologically the matured edition that might have been predicted of young Luther Burbank in his "teens."

The true chronicle of his early life will be of invaluable service to the cause of truth both in religion and science. It will demonstrate that "like produces like" —or near alike. How it will rouse and feed the ambition of the vast army of our young men and women to whom the doors of our universities are locked by the freaks of fortune!

Luther Burbank took greater pride in the days of his youth than in the days of his greatness. His face would light up with pleasure as he related how much March 7, 1849, as the date of his birth, and Lancaster, Massachusetts, as the place, meant to him—that he happened to be the thirteenth of fifteen children and didn't care—that his mother of ninety-seven years seems good evidence that maternity must be a friend of longevity—that a blend of English and Scotch in one's ancestry is worth while—that the "human plant in the cradle" in that Lancaster home was like all other feeders from the bottle and that it was puritanism in solution.

As he sprouted into boyhood, his young mind received and retained varied impressions from his environment with almost faultless powers of registration. Nothing seems to have escaped him; at least, after sixty years of incredible toil, he could analyze them one after another with scientific minuteness, as if they had happened yesterday.

He often spoke of a double inheritance handed down to him from his father. Thus he explains it: "There was a certain definiteness about all he did. I learned that this quality was based on absolute honesty toward everything met in life." That will explain his attitude toward religion. Not less important was the second half of this inheritance: "His firm belief in the power and value of method which exercised no mean influence upon my life from the start."

To the common schools of Lancaster, Massachusetts, and to a local academy, he was sent for the only classroom education that came into his boyhood life. Later he was privileged to take a course in medicine.

He was profoundly influenced, in the formative years of his life, by three men and three books. After a most careful analysis of the incidents of his boyhood days, it is my conviction that the secret of his success can be traced to those influences in combination.

Luther Burbank did not hesitate to attribute the most powerful of the early formative influences of his life to his association with an older cousin of his— Professor Levi Burbank. How his views of life were broadened and his methods of investigation reduced to a basis of scientific precision will be understood from his brief summary of the man: "My cousin was a man of parts. He had a strong bent toward biology, and he specialized in geology. His knowledge of plant life was profound. He had a true scientist's mind. His was strictly the scientific point of view. He avoided the technicalities of science, preferring to talk interestingly and simply of the world of Nature all about us."

For a time his cousin and he lived under the same roof and a strong and growing bond united them. Of their daily habits he thus speaks: "He took me out in the woods and fields and gave me a clear insight into the life going on in them that is so closely associated with ours. It was not alone the actual information I thus gained—though this was of the greatest value—but the point of view, the broad grasp of basic principles which were to him an open book, that hold their influence over me to this day."

Louis Agassiz (1807-73), professor of natural history at Harvard, was a close personal friend of Luther's father. In 1863, when Luther had attained his fourteenth year and Agassiz was just fifty-six years old, he formed his acquaintance, so that for ten precious years he sat at the feet of that great master.

Ralph Waldo Emerson (1803-82) was the third of the group that exercised a powerful influence over his young life. He recalled with remarkable distinctness, after the long interval of fifty-five years, many of his personal conversations with him.

"Three book influences," said Luther Burbank, "stand out in my life as having influenced greatly my career."

He was a close reader of the works of Henry David

Thoreau (1817-62), because he appealed to him as
the "naturalist who saw." In the writings of Friedrich
Alexander Humboldt (1769-1859) he discovered a
world of interest—"A wealth of fact, observation,
deduction and comment." Thus he expressed the
nature of his influence over him: "Perhaps the basic
thought I absorbed was the idealistic and intrinsic
worth of the work in which I was later to embark."

It was Charles Darwin (1809-82), however, "the
daring discoverer," who both by his brilliant career
and his published works exerted the most powerful
influence. Burbank found in him his master. Darwin
laid out the way that Burbank trod.

His *Animals and Plants under Domestication* threw
out a challenge that Burbank heard and accepted.
These are his words: "When, inspired by Darwin, I
began to grasp roughly the principles of variation—
that it is possible for man to train and change his
plants so as to meet his needs and desires—my career
was fixed—my path in life clearly indicated."

As he began to sense the message of that book, a
new light entered his soul which fired his ambition
by imaging before his mind the unborn possibilities
of the laws of variation, hastening the day when he
should experiment with those principles in far-off
California.

Up to this experience, Burbank's life had been
passed in much the same dull monotony as countless
other lives. He had worked in the Ames Plow Factory
at fifty cents a day. Market-gardening and seed raising in a small way kept him busy and led in 1873 to
the "Burbank potato" as the outcome of planting a

few promising seeds found in a seed boll of the Early Rose.

Yet there is a vital sense in which those days were the most important in his entire career. Again and again did he put the emphasis on this fact with all the intenseness of his nature. And had he not just reason?

In those days of priceless value he laid a foundation of good health, stored his mind with the facts discovered by the world's great naturalists, saw visions that fired his soul, dreamed of future conquests and panted for his opportunity. And it came.

The story of Luther Burbank's life as the man of science is unique in the formidable assembly of America's self-made great men. Once he trod the soil of California, the opportunities for plant breeding for which he had yearned unfolded to his uses with all the naturalness of one of his own most beautiful roses. In the course of fifty years, millions on millions of plants were grown by the deft hands of Luther Burbank. Of these millions, one plant is easily finer than all the others combined. It is the choicest, the most prolific, the most admired. It is Luther Burbank himself, who, duly transplanted from his native soil of New England, took deep root in the soil of California and produced a new and original variety of human character.

In those fifty years he made history, personal and scientific, that is only possible in our America. It is the essence of romance.

In 1875 Luther Burbank entered Santa Rosa, alone and unknown, with ten dollars, ten potatoes, a few choice books, one suit of clothes and a clean bill of health. In 1926 Luther Burbank owned several experimental tracts, among them one of thirteen acres of soil, known as the "Sebastopol Farm." In a country of boundless range like the Golden State, these holdings were, to be sure, mere specks of earth. Yet within that tiny acreage he so applied—to quote the words of Dr. David Starr Jordan—"our knowledge of heredity, selection and crossing to the development of plants that he stands unique in the world."

Of no other plot on God's green earth, of no other man in recorded history can these strong words of that highly qualified scientist be written. It took a long time, of course, for him to make this mark upon the world, so painfully slow to sense genius and so ungenerously slow to reward it. Not that Burbank cared. He at last became well known to the world as well as to men of science as a man "always interested in the phenomena of Nature and never seeking fame nor money nor anything else for himself."

Through fifty years of slow, tedious, painful climbing his love of science urged him on to the exercise of infinite patience, until his feet rested on a summit high above his fondest early hopes.

None will ever know how much Luther Burbank endured in those early years of California life. Alone and unaided, he started out in 1875, nursing his dream children. Penniless, he took the first job that offered itself, that of cleaning chicken coops. He slept inside one of them for a time, and was grateful, too, for its shelter. He knew the pangs of unsatisfied hunger. When serious sickness came, an old woman tended him, fed him on milk and saved his life.

There were still long years ahead of waiting, waiting, waiting. Oh, to possess just a few acres in which he might walk in spirit with Darwin amongst his plants, selecting, crossing, training! That was the essence of his dreams; and when that day came and he began to apply the great lessons of his masters, by slow degrees there came to fruition in his life the promise of his early teacher who bade him, "Learn to labor and to wait."

It takes no less than eight volumes of printed matter to contain even a summary of the work which he accomplished. Of the quality of that work, thus speaks Dr. Hugo De Vries of Amsterdam, Holland, one of the world's great naturalists: "Luther Burbank was the greatest breeder of plants the world has ever known. The magnitude of his work exceeds anything that was ever done before." At the hour of writing, there are over six thousand extensive experiments under way; there are now growing over five thousand distinct botanical specimens from all parts of the world; more than a million plants are raised every year for testing.

No man is more qualified to pass upon the life-work of Luther Burbank than David Starr Jordan. His standing in the scientific world, combined with his life-long intimacy with both Luther Burbank and his work, renders his criticism of unusual value.

Thus Jordan speaks:

Burbank's ways are Nature's ways, for Burbank differs from other men in this, that his whole life is given to the study of how Nature does things. His greatest service to science is to show what can be achieved through deeper knowledge of things as they are. He has shown the infinite variety of Nature as exhibited in the varying life and ways of the millions of kinds of living things. He has shown the unity of Nature in again demonstrating the final essential simplicity of creative processes. He has put into practical utility the teachings of his great master, Darwin, and he has enriched the world with thousands of fruits and flowers, useful and delightful, which but for him would have existed only among the conceivable possibilities of creation. He has helped mankind by increasing enormously the economic values of plant life. He has helped even more our science and our philosophy by his practical and successful tests of biologic theories.

Few tributes, as between one scientist and another, are more accurate in fact and generous in spirit.

When we pass from the things of Nature to the things of spirit, Luther Burbank admits us, as it were, into the sanctuary of his being. We become more and more conscious, as we take up our abode with him, of his deeply spiritual nature and the supersensitiveness of his soul. They form a mirror in which that popular error—assiduously cultivated and circulated by anti-evolutionists—that science is opposed to religion, suffers complete exposure.

Luther Burbank was equally at home in the kingdom of Nature and the kingdom of spirit. In a peculiar degree, he suggested the most perfect balance in his relation to both. It would be quite as absurd to call him a "mystic" in respect to his spiritual experiences as it is to call him a "wizard" in respect to his plant creations. But I have never known a man who was so free from rules, traditions and conventional beliefs and prejudices.

Things that would stagger the average man he took as a matter of course. Fearlessly he marched forward in his quest for truth, as if the supreme demand of things spiritual was whole-hearted response to the precept: "Prove all things; hold fast that which is good."

A careful study of the following features of his life-work and character will prepare the way for becoming rightly acquainted with the strong convictions that will be found expressed in succeeding pages.

Luther Burbank behaved just as naturally in dealing with the things of spirit as if he were studying his favorite plants. The impression invariably left upon my mind, at the end of a religious discussion with him, was that he looked upon things tangible as the shadows, and the things unseen as the eternal substance. Like the child of Nature in the midst of his plants and flowers, he "lived and moved and had his being" unafraid in the precincts of the invisible. One day he said to me with a smile: " 'Tis all so simple." He made his way about with the same sweetly trustful spirit in both kingdoms.

His motto was: *Omne vivum ex vivo*. When I put the question to him one day: "Can you possibly conceive of science as the breeder of agnosticism?" his answer was instant and direct: "No! No! Science is knowledge arranged and classified according to truth, facts and the general laws of Nature. Except through science there is no personal salvation, there is no national salvation. It is simply a crossing from things to the essence of things." What could more clearly demonstrate the simplicity with which the mind of the great scientist sensed the harmony existing in the relations between natural law and the spiritual world!

No man in history lived so long with Nature or gave to the world, as a result of such close companionship, so many rich and varied blessings. For more than sixty years his mind was concentrated on Nature's possibilities, intent on learning her secrets. To this study he brought naturally acute powers of observation, infinite patience and the most delicate discrimination in analysis. It can readily be seen how those qualities would develop and become perfected through the years. Alone amid the silences of Nature, he worked over the millions on millions of plants that passed through his hands. Profitable results of any kind depended upon an ability to detect in a flash variations that would pass most observers unnoticed.

Once, in speaking of the effect on things spiritual of this life-long detective work with plants, he said to me:

My theory of the laws and underlying principles of plant-creation is in many respects opposed to the theories of the materialists. I am a sincere believer in a higher power than man's. Every atom, every molecule, plant, animal or planet, is only an aggregation of organized unit forces, which, though teeming with inconceivable power, are held in equilibrium by stronger forces for a time. All life on our planet is, so to speak, just on the outer fringe of this infinite ocean of force. The universe is not half dead, but all alive.

It is not hard to reason that, when a man of native spiritual power spends a lifetime in such living relationship with Nature, his insight into the ways of the Infinite become penetrating and real.

Has he not earned a right to a respectful hearing when he says: "I prefer and claim the right to worship the infinite, everlasting, almighty God of this vast universe as revealed to us gradually, step by step, by the demonstrable truths of our savior, science."

In his attitude toward things spiritual I have never been in contact with a man so free from the bondage of tradition and the blinders of prejudice. He championed no system, held himself aloof so as to be free to pass by all structural theology on the other side and seek the truth, for truth's sake alone, with all the single-minded intenseness of his nature.

As delicate in physical build as an orchid, with a nature ever as sensitive as his plants to light and warmth, and a face reflecting serenity of mind, he lived at peace with himself and all the world.

"In how far did his belief express itself and bear fruit?" is a question often asked of me, and my reply is definite. For love, for unselfishness, for great services to humanity, for kindness, for sweet reasonableness and tolerance, for joyousness of living, for simplicity, for the splendor of his brilliant physical, mental and spiritual powers, pureness of life and character, he stands alone among the many thousands of other men I have met in a public life of over forty years.

Luther Burbank's is the one life known to me that was incomparably in tune with the Infinite.

It was the most natural thing in the world for him to exclaim: "I love sunshine, the blue sky, trees, flowers, mountains, green meadows, running brooks, the ocean waves softly rippling along the sandy beach or pounding the rocky cliffs with their thunder and roar, the birds of the field, waterfalls, the rainbow, the dawn, the noonday and the evening sunset—but children above them all."

Perhaps no man in our United States of America received more letters from little children than Luther Burbank. With the remarkable instinct of divination given to the child, they sensed and enjoyed his great love for them. Speaking of the young of the human species he once said: "The child is the most sensitive plant on earth; it will respond (by structural changes) to repetition just as a plant will; once fixed, a quality of spiritual power and a trait (of character) will stay with a child for ever."

Hundreds of schools throughout California combined in celebrating Luther Burbank's birthday. And the children on these occasions repeated the following standard of their young lives, as prepared by him:

Whom do you love among your schoolmates?
Not those who throw stones at innocent animals;

not those who break and destroy fences, trees and windows; not those who wish to quarrel and fight; but you do love and respect those who are kind, gentle and unselfish—the peacemakers.

Weakling cowards boast, swagger and brag; the brave ones, the good ones are gentle and kind.

Cultivate kind, gentle, loving thoughts toward every person and animal, and even plants, stars, oceans, rivers and hills. You will find yourself growing more happy each day, and with happiness comes health and everything you want.

One is reminded of the language of the apostle: "Little children, love one another."

Thus greatness and loving gentleness of soul blended in his capacious nature like the meeting of two oceans.

David Starr Jordan, in his summary of Burbank's rank in the realm of science, wrote thus of him: "If his place is outside the temple of science, there are not many of the rest of us who will be found fit to enter. . . . In his own way, Burbank belongs in the class of Faraday and the long array of self-taught great men who lived while the universities were spending their strength on fine points of grammar and hazy conceptions of philosophy."

After twenty years of close friendship with Burbank, during which I was honored with his closest confidence and the open confession of his religious opinions and beliefs, I can declare with equal confidence: "If his place is outside the temple of religion there are not many of the rest of us who will be found fit to enter. In his own way, Burbank belongs in the long

array of self-taught great men, who lived while
religious organizations were spending their strength
on fine points of theology and hazy conceptions of
God."

LETTER FROM LUTHER BURBANK TO HIS MOTHER

WORCESTER, April 25, 1869.

DEAR MOTHER:

I have been to meeting to-day and now have some spare time to write home. Have we not had two fine days to-day and yesterday? I have just been out picking a few flowers, but do not find the familiar may-flower.

Went to the drawing school yesterday afternoon and after supper went through the woods to a hill where all was quiet save the frogs in a distant pond and the joyous birds. I could see a great distance in every direction. The sun had just hidden his face beyond the far-off western horizon whose edges were tinged with silver and gold. I sat down upon a stump where the grass was green and enjoyed the pure air and the beautiful scene around me. Looking toward the south I could see the city spread before me; in the opposite direction was grand Wachusett which has about the same profile as when seen from Lancaster and nearer by were smaller hills, their sides just beginning to be clothed in the robe of summer and, between them, ponds as quiet and smooth as if frozen. It was a beautiful sight—I cannot describe it. My thoughts wandered over the past and future of this life which a bountiful God has given me to enjoy, and I thought: "Am I growing in anything which is noble, manly,

31

good or pure, or am I growing more beastly. Oh, is not life itself a great blessing; each of us poor sinful human beings have the privilege of elevating, improving, purifying and fitting for heaven these immortal minds of ours, or we may make them a thousand times worse than that of the groveling swine."

I take great pleasure in studying the hundreds of faces which I meet every day, no two of them look alike. It is easy to tell the high and the low, the good and the bad, and generally the rich and the poor; some of them always look pleasant, pure and happy; others dirty, mean and miserable.

Monday morning. My string was cut short last night by seeing that it was time to go to meeting. Uncle Nelson has been heard from direct in two ways, he is in Belfast, Maine, with his steamer, the "White Fawn." Aunt Jane has been up here two or three times lately. I think she is very well for her. I want very much to hear from you and Emma this week. Emma must not wait for Monday to write, but send me one Wed. too if she can afford it. When I was sitting on the hill Sat. night I might have said that I thought of a large brick house with a white Ell, and the friends thereabout twenty miles away. Hope you are all well and enjoying yourselves. We have not been paid off yet. The Co. owe me about $120. Let Emma write how she likes this mess of mental fodder and if the rhubarb is up, and if Trip [the dog] is well, etc.

I hope to hear from you soon. I enjoy reading letters from home pretty well. Yours with love

LUTHER.

Monday noon.   Joe Stone (the Groton Mill River Stone) has been in here several days lately at court— he came in to see me last week.   Uncle Hiram is in Maine.   Have not heard from Dr. Willis yet.   I have a tooth which ought to be attended to and have half a mind to come home Saturday night and come in with you Tuesday, Probate day.   Hope to hear from you this week.   With love

LUTHER.

A CHALLENGE TO THOUGHT

In one of his busiest mornings late in the month of January, 1926, Luther Burbank graciously granted an interview to a young reporter of a local paper. Out of the goodness of his heart he dropped his work amongst his bulbs to do the young man a favor. In the few minutes available, he was asked for a definite answer to a question dealing with the subject of immortality. Burbank, in the course of his reply, called himself an "infidel." The quick, enterprising mind of the youth pictured the splendid front-page headline which that word would make. His vision was unerring. That ugly word, so suggestive of the lack of religion, or worse, was tagged to the religious life of Luther Burbank and flashed across both continent and ocean. Once in motion it got beyond control, and in a short time some eight thousand American and foreign newspapers and magazines strengthened an alliance between them at once odious and untrue.

It is not difficult to anticipate the inevitable result. At a season of the year when his work as a naturalist demanded every moment of his time, he was forced to undergo the most exciting and harassing experiences of his entire career. Poor Luther Burbank, who never injured a fellow mortal in his more than seventy years, the gentlest, purest, kindliest of men, was made the object of a narrow, bitter religious war of words. He who delighted to live a life of ascetic solitude amongst his plants and flowers was made a public spectacle. His name was linked with the aggressive unbelief of Ingersoll, and men and women whispered it in the same breath with those of Tom Paine and Charles Bradlaugh. His neat study was turned into a litter of letters. In his home town of Santa Rosa, this friend of little children, this champion of the poor and the afflicted, was pestered by women of the several evangelical churches, who had formed groups of praying circles to supplicate their God that He might grant the deluded and benighted Burbank light, repentance and forgiveness. His home was besieged by self-appointed representatives of the "faithful," who implored him to recant. The tragedy of Dayton, Tennessee, was reënacted in Santa Rosa, California. He who had reveled for sixty years in the silences of Nature was now compelled to spend his days amid the angry tumult of incarnated fanaticism. Like Paul of old, he was to learn what men who "fought with beasts at Ephesus" felt while the fight was going on. When we met at that time, the expression which he wore was that of a man who had been buffeted by "the petrified hypocrisy" of men and women whose ideas of religion made it possible for them to bless and curse in the same breath.

In the midst of that awful experience, many invitations came to him to occupy church pulpits to help allay the seething feelings of narrow bigots. Finally he was persuaded to accept one of them from the greatest Sunday audience that assembles in the city of San Francisco, and on the last Sunday in January he deliv-

ered in the First Congregational Church an address
that has since become historic. The seating capacity
of the church is two thousand people, but on that
morning more than twenty-five hundred people lis-
tened to him with breathless attention. In the congre-
gation were bankers, lawyers, merchants, teachers and
representatives of almost every shade of religious
belief known in the cosmopolitan city of San Francisco, among them hundreds who had perhaps not
attended church service for many years.

We chatted together before the hour of service and
I was conscious of what a nervous strain he was under.
Dr. James L. Gordon, the broad-minded pastor, wel-
comed him in a true, loving spirit, and with spoken
words of strength and tolerance. Just before he rose
I whispered friendly wishes, and he smiled as he turned
to face that vast concourse.

There was something strangely fascinating about
the man as he stood there. His clear, thin voice filled
that vast auditorium. Frail in form, with pale face
and classic head, no man, I will venture to say, ever
stood on that spot whose personality suggested such
startling contrasts. It seemed to me as if a prophet
had sprung to life out of the ages. Knowing his dread
of public functions, his shyness and reserve, I followed
his opening sentences, my own throat tight with mis-
giving. But I was soon made to realize that he more
than measured up to the requirements of the occasion.
As he went on with slow, almost hesitating speech, a
stillness like unto death came over the great audience,
and men and women hung upon every word he uttered
in a kind of spell.

His opening sentence launched out into the deep. "I love everybody. I love everything. I love especially to look into the deep, worshipful, liquid eyes of Bonita, my dog, whose devotion is as profound as life itself. But better yet, I love to look into the fearless, honest, trusting eyes of a child who so long has been said by theologians to be conceived and born in sin and pre-damned at birth."

His entire message was pitched in the same keys of love and joy.

Not in the history of churches in any city of the Golden State has the scene that followed ever been paralleled. Hundreds pressed in upon him at the close of the service and waited patiently for the chance of grasping his hand and blessing him for his words. They had proved, indeed, "a challenge to thought for those who were asleep," and struck some of the divinest chords in the strange symphony of life.

LUTHER BURBANK'S ADDRESS

*Delivered in the First Congregational Church,
San Francisco*

"I love everybody! I love everything! Some
people seem to make mistakes, but everything and
everybody has something of value to contribute or
they would not be here.

"I love humanity, which has been a constant delight
to me during all my seventy-seven years of life; and
I love flowers, trees, animals and all the works of
Nature as they pass before us in time and space. What
a joy life is when you have made a close working
partnership with Nature, helping her to produce
for the benefit of mankind new forms, colors and
perfumes in flowers which were never known before;
fruits in form, size, color and flavor never before seen
on this globe; and grains of enormously increased productiveness, whose fat kernels are filled with more and
better nourishment, a veritable storehouse of perfect
food—new food for all the world's untold millions
for all time to come.

"All things—plants, animals and men—are already
in eternity traveling across the face of time, whence
we know not, whither who is able to say. Let us have
one world at a time and let us make the journey one

of joy to our fellow passengers and just as convenient and happy for them as we can, and trust the rest as we trust life.

"Let us read the Bible without the ill-fitting colored spectacles of theology, just as we read other books, using our own judgment and reason, listening to the voice, not to the noisy babble without. Most of us possess discriminating reasoning powers. Can we use them or must we be fed by others like babes?

"I love especially to look into the deep, worshipful, liquid eyes of Bonita, my dog, whose devotion is as profound and lasting as life itself. But better yet, I love to look into the fearless, honest, trusting eyes of a child who so long has been said by theologians to be conceived and born in sin and pre-damned at birth. Do you believe all our teachers without question? I cannot. We must 'prove all things' and 'hold fast that which is good.'

"What does the Bible mean when it distinctly says, 'By their fruits ye shall know them'? Works count far more than words with those who think clearly.

"Euripides long ago said, 'Who dares not speak his free thought is a slave.' I nominated myself as an 'infidel' as a challenge to thought for those who are asleep. The word is harmless if properly used. Its stigma has been heaped upon it by unthinking people who associate it with the bogie devil and his malicious works. The devil has never concerned me, as I have always used my own conscience, not the dictum of any cult.

"If my words have awakened thought in narrow bigots and petrified hypocrites, they will have done their appointed work. The universal voice of science tells us that the consequences fall upon ourselves here and now, if we misuse this wonderful body, or mind, or the all-pervading spirit of good. Why not accept these plain facts and guide our lives accordingly? We must not be deceived by blind leaders of the blind, calmly expecting to be 'saved' by anyone except by the Kingdom within ourselves. The truly honest and brave ones know that if they are to be saved it must be by their own efforts. The truth hurts for a while as do the forceps that remove an old, useless tooth, but health and happiness may be restored by the painful removal of the disturbing member.

"My mother, who lived to the ripe old age of ninety-seven years, used very often in my boyhood and youthful days to say, 'Luther, I wish you to make this world a better place to live in than it was before you lived.' I have unfailingly tried all of my own long life to live up to this standard. I was not told to believe this or that or be damned.

"I reiterate: The religion of most people is what they would like to believe, not what they do believe, and very few stop to examine its foundation underneath. The idea that a good God would send people to a burning hell is utterly damnable to me—the ravings of insanity, superstition gone to seed! I don't want to have anything to do with such a God. I am a lover of man and of Christ as a man and his work, and all things that help humanity; but nevertheless, just as he was an infidel then, I am an infidel to-day. I prefer and claim the right to worship the infinite, everlasting, almighty God of this vast universe as revealed to us gradually, step by step, by the demonstrable truths of our savior, science.

"Do you think Christ or Mohammed, Confucius, Baal or even the gods of ancient mythology are dead? Not so. Do you think Pericles, Marcus Aurelius, Moses, Shakespeare, Spinoza, Aristotle, Tolstoi, Franklin, Emerson are dead? No. Their very personality lives and will live forever in our lives and in the lives of all those who will follow us. All of them are with us to-day. No one lives who is not influenced, more or less, by these great ones according to the capacity of the cup of knowledge which they bring to these ever-flowing fountains to be filled.

"Olive Schreiner says: 'Holiness is an infinite compassion for others; greatness is to take the common things of life, and walk truly among them.

" 'All things on earth have their price; and for truth we pay the dearest. We barter it for love and sympathy. The road to honor is paved with thorns; but on the path to truth at every step you set your foot down on your own heart.

" 'For the little soul that cries aloud for continued personal existence for itself and its beloved, there is no help. For the soul which knows itself no more as a unit, but as a part of the Universal Unity of which the beloved also is a part, which feels within itself the throb of the Universal Life—for that soul there is no death.' "

THE RESULT OF THE CHALLENGE

Both new and startling were the experiences that happened to Luther Burbank as the direct result of his "Challenge to Thought." For the first time in his long career of fifty years he had entered the realm of religious discussion, with a statement of his beliefs delivered with a frankness and precision of thought characteristic of the man. Viewing the aftermath of his utterance from the human standpoint alone, it had all the elements of tragedy. The center of gravity of his personality was suddenly transferred from the peace and quietness of his horticultural labors into the vortex of a religious controversy. No man, in my experience of forty years of public life, was less fitted to grapple with such an acute and unforeseen situation. Gentle, loving, of retiring habits, he had lived for fifty years in his California home amongst his plants and flowers, at peace with his God, with himself, with all the world. While I was preparing a sketch of his scientific career during the month of October, 1925, we were brought into close companionship. His charm as a man of settled calm, of peaceful serenity of spirit and of joyousness of being was the chief impression he made upon me. Then at the summit of his success in the world of science, he bore his honors with a rare modesty. It is easy of belief that such a spirit would shrink with horror from the publicity and strife of a religious controversy. Nothing could have been more abhorrent to his kindliness of nature.

His public statement was exploited by the press, broadcasted by radio, and made the topic of innumerable religious discourses throughout the country. The consequence was a flood of letters and telegrams from all parts of the world. For many weeks I assisted him in reading and assorting these thousands of letters. Science has turned our world into a small family dwelling place. From Australia and New Zealand cables were received, requesting permission to publish his "message."

They were all brought to his study, which was small and compact, and filled with literature on every possible subject. On the wall over the bookcase in a frame hung a poem, in clear, strong print, as follows:

Oft as in solitude and shade I wander,
  Through the green aisles, or stretched upon the sod;
Awed by the silence, reverently I ponder
  The ways of God.

Your voiceless lips of flowers are preachers,
  Each cup a pulpit—each leaf a book—
Supplying to my fancy numerous teachers,
  From lowliest nook.

Floral apostles, that in dewdrop splendor
  Weep without woe, and blush without a crime,
O may I learn, and ne'er surrender
  Your love sublime.

Over Luther Burbank's desk a face looked down with a massive head and the strong eye of the true scholar—that of Dr. David Starr Jordan. Once

Burbank remarked, as we gazed upon it: "One of the strongest minds of our nation."

In the days that followed, the floor was piled up each morning with the incoming mail, like a huge catch of fish out of the net. Burbank sat in the center of his study, paper-knife in hand. Each letter was opened with neatness and minimum effort, glanced through or read even more carefully, decided upon, and then returned to its envelope. His face throughout was a study, and he would often whisper a word of criticism to me. In the weeks we thus spent together some nine thousand letters passed through his hands, letters from every state in the Union, from Canada, and from greater distances.

It may safely be asserted that their contents struck every string in the gamut of human nature. It was hard to conceive that Nature could be so diverse or religion become so distorted.

Throughout it all the self-control of Luther Burbank was remarkable. There were times when I sensed a disturbed look—the expression of a man who fought hard to master his emotions. He was commended, rebuked, scolded, assailed, chided, praised, cursed and blessed. And those letters came from every type of citizen. They were written by presidents of universities, scientists, clergymen, physicians, lecturers, laborers, journalists, cranks, business men, lawyers, judges, inmates of asylums and young men and young women, all pouring out their sentiments, opinions and beliefs with frankness and spontaneity, moved to do so, some of them, by the spirit of kindness, and others, by a very passion of brutality.

Burbank's attitude toward the entire correspondence was marked by the qualities of thoroughness
and patience responsible for his success in the scientific world. There were days when I could have
burnt all the piles of letters in one bonfire, out of a
realization that the strain upon his strength was becoming abnormal and that the logical end would be a
disordered nervous condition. No tangible result of
a constructive character could possibly be disentangled from such a mass of discordant elements.
But it was Burbank's firm determination to "see it
through," and he struggled on with a manly fortitude.

Modernists, fundamentalists, agnostics, atheists,
Ethical Culturists, Jews, Catholics, Protestants,
Spiritualists, heretics, Mormons and a score of other
partisans poured out upon his head the convictions
and conclusions of their minds without restraint.

Hundreds of letters from young men and women,
describing their doubts and spiritual struggles and
pleading for light, were read with the utmost care and
laid aside for a personal response. "This is heartbreaking," he would often whisper as he lingered over a
letter, underlining certain passages in it. Many an
appeal brought tears to his eyes, as he confessed his
helplessness. "I'm a member of a club in which every
one of us is a practical unbeliever," wrote a student
of an Eastern college. "Why try to pray when we
don't know whether God is, in this jumble of mis-
beliefs?" was the final sentence of a letter in which a
young man bared the doubts of his soul. A Baptist
minister of Kansas City, who was cast out of his
church for publicly endorsing Burbank's statement of

belief, wrote to say how he rejoiced at his new freedom from dogmatic domination and the right he had asserted to think as his mind and conscience demanded. From a young man in Virginia, engaged in horticulture, came an appeal that affected Burbank visibly. In the heart of the country, with few friends, the loss of his mother had brought the greatest sorrow into his soul. He wrote: "What does religion offer me in these days of awful darkness—is there a hope that may sustain me? Is God a reality? I don't know which way to turn."

In the midst of letters breathing despair a letter of love and hope would often supply an antidote of the greatest possible strength and comfort. From Ina Coolbrith, California's poetess laureate, for example, came her *Songs from the Golden State* and the following inscription from her pen: "TO OUR 'BELOVED INFIDEL' LUTHER BURBANK, whose every act through life has been one Faith. With unfailing faith from Ina Coolbrith." Many letters came from toilers, containing blunt, frank statements that rejoiced his heart. "Good luck to you, dear friend Burbank," wrote a miner from an Eastern state; "let's have the truth at all costs. Self and family has quit church going till a man comes along who will give us a god of love and forget about hell fire."

Of the hundreds of abusive letters the following two may be accepted as fitting examples: "Dear Sir: One Bryan is worth a million Burbanks to any world, and the Bible will be doing business when you and your flowers are blowing down the years. Abilene, Kansas." "Dear Sir: You will be held responsible for your statement. You have set aside the Bible, made the God of the Bible a liar, made Jesus Christ an impostor. Thus you declare yourself to be a heathen. It is too bad you have so little sense. Keokuk, Iowa."

Many of the most sympathetic letters were received from the universities of the land. They were examples of a breadth of thought that cheered him beyond the power of language to describe. His close friendship for Dr. W. Ray Lyman Wilbur, President of Stanford University, made the sentiment of the following letter very real to him: "Dear Mr. Burbank—I hope your usual equanimity is not being disturbed by the HOWLERS. Anyone who compels thought as you have is a real contribution to us all. Faithfully yours."

In the same spirit wrote Mrs. Henrietta B. Lindsey, in the name of her husband: "Denver. My dear Mr. Burbank—Judge Lindsey is just leaving on an emergency trip. Thanks for your brave attempt to make people think. Sincerely."

The writer of the following is nationally well known: "Being an admirer of yours for years past in your researches and diligence with patience combined, I cannot help but admire your opinion on the reincarnation and super-existence of Jesus, whom all students realize was a Jewish student-preacher. The orthodox Jew does not recognize His divinity, as they have the history as it transpired, and I am pleased to see that you, in your wisdom, have the courage to come out against those who know not."

With a sweet smile, Burbank handed me a letter from a mother of many children, in which not a word contained the suggestion of a religious discussion. It

simply stated that a box, containing choice tidbits for
his dog companion "Bonita" had been shipped, adding
that his loving reference to his dog in his San Francisco
address had touched her heart.

One man, to mark his despair and in mockery of
every semblance of hope, enclosed the following passage from the pen of Lord Balfour: "His [man's] very
existence is an accident; his story a brief and discredit-
able episode in the life of one of the meanest of the
planets." As Burbank put it down, he made the
observation that the writer must have been in very
"poor health."

"Isn't it just splendid to get at the exact truth?"
writes a New Yorker. "The physical strength of a
healthy ape is three times that of a human being, and
the mental strength three times that of an evolu-
tionist."

The longest letters invariably were the letters of
abuse, couched in coarse language. Without exception
they were based on the narrowest interpretation of
religion and filled with biblical quotations. Illiteracy
and bigotry went hand in hand. Texts of Scripture,
full of love, were most incongruously asked to serve
as auxiliaries to sentences of bitter hatred.

Only once, throughout all the weeks we were sift-
ing, reading and arranging this correspondence, did
he seem to be filled with righteous indignation. From
a minister in Pasadena came the following statement,
with its disrespectful form of salutation: "Burbank—
Lovers of Christ recently winced and staggered under
the blasphemous attacks made by seventy-seven-year-

old Luther Burbank, nationally famous plant wizard. He declared, among other things, 'Heaven and earth is a myth and a mockery, despite what the Bible says. Man needs no Salvation; he is his own Savior.' Mr. Burbank should stay in his own field, as a horticulturist. He is thoroughly at home and probably the best in the nation. But when he steps into the foreign (to him) element of theology, he is more ignorant than the veriest babe in Christ among you; his teaching on 'Eternal Life' is not even as valuable as John D. Rockefeller on 'How to Play Football.'

"We ministers do not go into his laboratories and inform the world that he is in error regarding many of his findings; and, as he admits he is not a Christian, he should in all courtesy realize he is out of his realm.

"He has gathered to his banner hundreds of Christ's enemies, some of whom had been afraid to come out in the open. Unitarians, scientists, etc., who have always belittled Christ, are with him. But God is not mocked, and I tremble for them at the result, while I pity and pray for the man who is closing a great career as a poor, deluded dupe of the Devil."

After a long silence, Luther Burbank opened his private drawer and, extracting a Bible, handed it to me. "That," said he, "with the letter that accompanied it, is the most treasured of anything that came to me as a result of this whole discussion." It was a family Bible, an Oxford edition, well worn and marked, with the clearest of type on "Ceylon paper." The letter was written by a woman of evident culture, who expressed her pride in asking his acceptance of the one thing she valued most in life and thanked him for his bold stand for a religion disentangled from the meshes of superstition.

Of the communications received by Burbank from clergymen throughout the country one of those that seemed most to appeal to him was written by the pen of Dr. E. Morgan Isaac, a Congregational pastor. "Luther Burbank," said he, "has declared to the world that he is religious. He would not so state it, perhaps, but we have his own word for it. He says, 'I love everybody. I love everything.' That sounds like the Man of Galilee. It is the very essence of true religion. Would to goodness all professed Christians were as religious as this heretic! The heretic is often the man who sees the soul of religion and loves that inner kingdom of power, but cares little or nothing for the extremes. He has discovered that the essence of religion is a spiritual atmosphere. It is the attitude of the soul to the unseen Presence that fills the universe and that may be seen in all expressions of life. He finds all theories of religion utterly inadequate to state the truth—indeed they harass his spirit, but he cannot conceive of the Infinite Beauty of life and love and power confined to a theological mold or statement of creed.

"He must have largeness, horizons that ever recede, life that the mind cannot measure, light that knows no darkness.

"His love goes out to all—life expression—for to him all is beautiful with the very presence of the Infinite.

"Again he says, 'Let us have one world at a time and let us make the journey one of joy to our fellow passengers, and just as convenient and happy for them as we can, and trust the rest as we trust life.'

"Luther Burbank has evidently caught some of this vision. He says: 'I prefer and claim the right to worship the infinite, everlasting almighty God of this vast universe as revealed to us gradually, step by step, by the demonstrable truths of our savior, science.' This seems shocking to many good people. But why? Because their thought has been cast in a certain kind of mold, the outstanding characteristic of which is limitation and fear. They are sure that all of revelation is in the Bible. The scientist sees an omnipresent God in Nature, and here the scientist has good company.

" 'Consider the lilies of the field how they grow. Behold the birds of the air that they sow not, neither do they reap, nor gather into barns, and your Heavenly Father feedeth them.'

"To Jesus all life was radiant with the presence of God—every child, every individual, the unfortunate, the outcast, the despised publican—all found in him a friend. He was a rough-weather friend as well as a friend of the calm day.

"Burbank would suit Jesus. A church with a thousand Burbanks would be a great church."

An old friend, full of culture and deep religious convictions, sent the following acrostic, which Luther Burbank specially requested should be included in this book of reminiscences of his religious experiences and beliefs.

I mmortal words to clarion notes,
N o minor chords of woe;
F ull from the deep of the Great All Source,
I n cleansing waves they flow.
D uty dies, love takes its place;
E ach soul is loosed from sin;
L ife again stands clean and strong in the Temple of God
　　within.

As the days and weeks passed, it was evident that the prolonged strain was telling upon him. To be taken from the open, with its warmth and sunshine, and forced to live, like a transplanted flower, within four walls was no ordinary trial to a man of Luther Burbank's habits.

Yet the physical change was nothing compared with the mental shock caused by the revelation of broken hearts, shattered beliefs and disappointed hopes. These were torment to his spiritual nature. Letters from young men in heady revolt against "the discovered deceptions and illusions of superstitions" pained and upset him greatly. Hundreds of those notes expressed the anxious desire to learn what the writers might put in the place of rejected myths which would satisfy their longing. And he felt so utterly helpless. Frequently he would retire to an adjoining room to rest upon the sofa. And during those days that the storm and tempest expressed in these thousands of communications caused him to tremble as an old oak of the forest, travelers from all parts of the world were knocking at his gate to seek an interview.

Before I close this chapter, let me transcribe a memo from his pen that will be found in a nook at the side of his desk:

How can you expect to have all children reared in love? By working to that end with vast patience upon the great body of the people—this great mingling of races—to teach such of them as do not love their children to love them, and to surround them with all the influence of love. This will not be universally accomplished to-day or to-morrow, and it may need centuries; but, if we are ever to advance in that direction and attain to this higher race, now is the time to begin the work—this very day. It is the part of every human being who comprehends the importance of this attitude toward children to bend all his energies in its promotion.

Love must be the basis of all our work for the race. Not gush, not mere sentimentality, *but abiding love which outlasts death.*

You can never bring up a child to its best estate without love.

One day, as we rested from our discussions, I took from the papers on his desk the following statement from his friend, David Starr Jordan, and read it to him:

Every robust human life is a life of faith, not faith in what other men have said or thought or dreamed of life, or death, or fate; not faith that some one afar off or long ago held a key to the riddle of existence, which is not ours to fashion or to hold; not faith in mystic symbolisms which only a priest may interpret.

Let us say rather, faith that there is in the

universe some force or spirit which transcends humanity, but of which the life of man is part, not the whole, something which is intensely real and which it is well for men to recognize, for to follow its ways brings effort and action, peace and helpfulness, the sole basis of happiness.

At the close of the reading, he smiled and said: "Yes! Such a faith belongs to the Religion of Humanity!"

Having shared with Burbank the reading of the great mass of letters that passed through our hands, I penned the following impressions one day, and he was in hearty agreement with me:

1. The bitterest letters were written by men and women who professed to be Christians.

2. The kindest letters were written by scientists and men and women of university training.

3. The longest letters were written by the illiterate.

4. The shortest letters were written by the cultured.

5. The most hopeful letters were written by men and women in agreement with the beliefs of Burbank.

6. The most pessimistic letters were written by fundamentalists.

7. The most abusive letters were written by those who assured Burbank they were praying for his soul's welfare.

8. At least eighty per cent of the writers found an appeal to which they could respond in the spirit of his message.

Glancing one day over the pages of the "Visitors'

Book," I copied, at haphazard, the following names of guests at his home. They are interesting, as indicating the varied type of life that came in contact with his and broadened his horizon: William Jennings Bryan, who wrote after his name, "In the home of one to whom Nature has whispered many of her secrets"; Jernando Senoza Vivas, Central America; Arnold E. V. Richardson, Melbourne, Victoria, Australia; Herbert Myrick, Springfield, Mass., who wrote, "What an interpreter you are of Nature's creative power"; Dr. Victor Reyes, La Paz, Bolivia; J. F. Ward, President, Department of Agriculture, Tasmania; George Edwin Baker, Director General of Posts, Peking, China; Dr. M. M. Paravians, Switzerland; Ed Diaz, Guatemala, Central America; P. J. Cramer, Buitenzorg, Java; Q. J. Wilansky, Jaffa, Palestine; F. A. Pezet, Lima, Peru; Wadaw Sieroszewski, Warsaw, Poland; Lydia M. Rogers, London, England.

R. E. Fisher (Major), Matania, Upper Egypt; R. D. Koch, Capetown, South Africa; A. Sodri, Rio de Janeiro, Brazil; Samuel Mendelssohn, Jerusalem, Palestine, who added "Meet me there."

David Starr Jordan of Stanford University, who wrote, "A perennial joy to see Burbank"; M. Th. Goethe, nephew of "the Goethe," Geisenheim, Germany; President John H. Wilson of St. Andrews University, Scotland; Lionel Hanlon, Whangarai, New Zealand.

Ella Wheeler Wilcox and Robert Wilcox; Professor J. P. Leotsakos, Lakonia, Greece; J. H. Duyvense, Jr., Amsterdam; Elinor Glyn, Sheering Harbor, Essex, who added, "The light that will light the world";

Carlo Umbrosol, Como, Italy; George W. Oliver, Washington, D. C.; P. G. Norberg, Goleberg, Sweden.

Dr. Arturo Spozio, Milano, Italy; Carlo Camacho, Director of Pathological Education, Santiago, Chile; Pablo Hoffmann, Mexico; James Bryce (Lord Bryce) of Oriel College, Oxford; E. Marion Bryce; Benjamin Ide Wheeler, Berkeley; Elbert Hubbard, Alice Hubbard, New York City; Dr. Tschemratx, Vienna, Austria.

John Burroughs, West Point, N. Y.; J. Watase, Tokyo, Japan; S. Vrooman, Fehoe, India; George Sterling, who added, "Most great men are doing more harm than good—not you"; A. Kolpin Rawn, Copenhagen, Denmark; Charles Ernest Lofthus, Norway; James Daly, Board of Agriculture, Dublin; Dionisius Roodsiuski, Moscow, Russia; F. J. Harper, Platkop, South Africa; Jose C. Zelston, San Jose, Costa Rica; Count Ferdinand Nermes, Budapest, Hungary.

Ambassador Juan Vignoli, Montevideo, Uruguay; Dr. George von Wendt, Finland; J. de Argoleo, Jr., Paris, France; Koka Fuur Vaman, Bombay, India; Vell Savich, Tiflis, Caucasus; Varaji Rajaram, Kolhapur, India.

Thomas A. Edison, Henry Ford, Clara J. Ford, Edsel B. Ford, H. S. Firestone; Opie Read, Chicago; Dr. J. W. Macfarlane, Pittsburgh. In the midst of his busiest days, Luther Burbank entertained Mr. and Mrs. Walter Martin of London, England, who motored from Los Angeles, Cal., to extend their hearty sympathy with "the spirit of his brave utterance."

Scientists gladly accept any new truth which can be demonstrated by experiment that is proven by the very laws of the cosmos not so with any new conception of religion these are fought with persecution and all the venom of the wild beasts of the jungle for many of the religious beliefs when literally carried into practice would bring humanity to the old jungle ideas and practices Ignorance of the truth is the only unpardonable sin which inevitably brings its dupes to ~~effect~~ fear and ~~stupe~~ superstition misery because it is too hard work to think and it is so much easier to be mental parasites allowing others to feed us thus being led astray by designing deceivers or self deceivers who may be as blind to truth as are their dupes.

SAMPLE OF LUTHER BURBANK'S HANDWRITING.

HIS RELIGION OF HUMANITY

For many years the home of Luther Burbank was a kind of Mecca to which men and women from all parts of the globe were attracted. Their visits were inspired by deep, personal interest in the man, his life-work and the world-wide fame that his success in science had created for him.

Of the hundreds on thousands who have thus made this pilgrimage, few have left without catching a modicum of the spirit of love and peace that abided there. It saturated his personality and grew more intense with the years.

His home reminded one of the villas nestling in the slopes of Perugia, that garden spot of Italy. It is embosomed in a settled serenity, comparable to the composure accompanying the silent growth of the plants and flowers.

But this serenity was by no means the offspring of ease and leisure.

Work to Luther Burbank was prayer in action. There was not, perhaps, a busier man in the State of California. The public does not know that in recent years few men have had better opportunities of studying the human plant in more varied forms. Letters arrived daily, often in the hundreds, seeking information as to his scientific work, his philosophy of life, his religious opinions and beliefs. There was always a stream of correspondence, from all parts of the world, requiring personal attention. Add to those duties the daily procession of visitors, and his unselfish willingness to meet them whenever possible, and it is plain to see how that quiet home became, in truth, a very beehive of industry.

Knowledge of this background is needed to understand the following exchange of letters between two close and life-long friends.

On September 21, 1925, Thomas A. Edison thus wrote to him:

> Friend Burbank: I hope you are not thinking of stopping work. It would be dangerous to your health. In a normal body, not injured by excesses, the mind is clear and more efficient as age increases, up to the end. I myself am approaching eighty. My mind is more active than ever. My body and all its parts are, of course, getting gray-headed, so to speak. I notice that I am getting awkward and my hearing is growing poor, but I still work eighteen hours a day at what I like and I enjoy it immensely.
>
> Very sincerely yours,
>
> THOS. A. EDISON.

In reply to this youthful and tireless worker, Burbank answered:

> My dear, wonderful Edison: Your kind and greatly appreciated letter received. The news-

papers seem to be over-ambitious to place me on the retired list. No, my dear Mr. Edison, I have never had a thought of stopping work, have more interest in my work than ever before, enjoy the pursuit of knowledge and work better than ever before. Every muscle in my body is as supple as ever, but I cannot apply myself to such long hours of hard physical labor as I used to, but am always up and at work at 6:30 in the morning. The inspiration of the early part of the day is superlative. It is a pity that I cannot dispose of my Sebastopol place without so much fuss, just to save time and give a little more attention to my extremely interesting Santa Rosa experiments. This, of course, does not require a reply or even to be read by such a busy man as you are. With profound admiration, love and esteem for yourself, and Mrs. Edison, I am always,

Faithfully yours,

LUTHER BURBANK.

And the spirit that permeated and controlled this daily schedule was so compact of living patience and kindly courtesy that it seemed to inform his body and mind with the buoyancy of youth.

After her return to her Eastern home, Helen Keller published a remarkable account of her visit to Burbank, replete with human interest. This noble woman, blind and deaf and dumb, related with all the accuracy of a master mind how she had seen Luther Burbank, heard his voice and imaged in her mind the love and gentleness of his personality.

My experiences in the home of Burbank taught me how the simple, trustful spirit of an earnest seeker after truth forms the major part of the equipment of the truly great scientist. They revealed, as naught else in a long ministry spent in large cities, how potent a force for good the spirit of love, of sweet tolerance, of human sympathy can be recognized to be by all sorts and conditions of men.

His philosophy of life, his personal opinions and beliefs on the vital relationship of science to religion, in which I was privileged to share his deepest convictions, have done more to consolidate my faith than any other one of the human contacts of my entire ministry.

His heart and soul were filled with sympathy for the millions of young men and young women chafing under the fetters of false tradition, their intelligence shocked by man-made creeds and false systems of belief. His one supreme desire was to revive within them a hope and love crushed by superstitious falsehoods, and put them in the way of a philosophy of life that would nourish their lives on the sunshine and joy of truth.

Only in that light may the opinions and beliefs that follow be understood aright.

Burbank's choice of the term "infidel," to express his attitude toward structural theology, aroused an interest more than nation-wide, confirming his belief that religion is a most vital force in the lives of the people. There is a conscious need of spiritual power to guide and strengthen men and women in an age of great doubt, of lawlessness and discontent. In the light of advanced science, he was convinced that heart and mind were never more receptive, provided truth is interpreted in terms of reason. He warned against forgetting the essential condition—in terms of reason. None knew better than he how foolish it would be to minimize that yearning after something that will plant love and hope in the heart. Science, he believed, has been a mighty force in paving the way for this reception of a reasonable religious life. Mere ethical codes have failed; humanity needs a religion to mold human conduct, draw out the noblest that is in us, and, above all, bring us into the living consciousness of the great Creative Force.

In analyzing this great mass of letters and telegrams from all parts of the world, the deepest impression made upon Burbank's mind was that structural theology had broken down. The writers of those nine thousand letters and telegrams from all over the world told their own story. What a harrowing picture of doubts, fears and despair they presented on the part of those who have severed themselves from institutional religion and find themselves adrift like hopeless castaways! Men and women want a God as never before, but not the God falsely interpreted by man-made theologies. More than eighty per cent of them turned out to be earnest seekers yearning for a religion free from the meshes of superstition, worn-out medievalism and false beliefs. Those young men and women bared their very souls in confession of their failure to get the slightest comfort or strength or hope from such a religion, and how they thirsted for a religion that would satisfy their needs! They prove that preserving the integrity of our minds intact is of infinitely more value than a mere adherence to any creed or system.

Burbank rejoiced that in his San Francisco address he had nominated himself an "infidel," as a challenge to thought for those who are asleep. He said in that address: "The word is harmless if properly used. Its stigma has been heaped upon it by unthinking people who associate it with the bogie devil and his malicious works. I am a lover of man and of Christ as a man, and his work, and all things that help humanity; but nevertheless, just as he was an infidel then, I am an infidel to-day." When Christ, he added, dared to face the false teachers of his day, those self-righteous formalists, and exposed their pseudo doctrines and hypocrisies, he was denounced by them as an unbeliever. They gnashed upon him with their teeth. They accused him of "casting out devils through Beelzebub, the prince of devils." They called him a madman. The stigma of infidelism represented only a part of their bitter hatred. No man in the history of the world was a greater infidel than Christ in relation to the errors of the day in which he lived.

When I pictured to Burbank the great and growing constituency who are disgusted and bitterly disappointed at the stupid superstitions, the narrow bigotry and hateful spirit kept alive under the name of religion, so vigorously championed by fundamentalists, he said that it was all absurd and illogical and benighted, that the term itself is a misnomer. Fundamentalism, as a word, implies intelligence; whereas it is employed to represent organized ignorance. The so-called fundamentalist flouts the truth of evolution, attests his belief in the verbal and literal inspiration of the Bible, blinds his eyes to the frequent errors of text and alleged fact, proclaims man's total depravity, insists that he was both conceived and born in sin, paints a fantastic heaven, consigns the unconverted sinner to a damnable hell-fire of eternal torment, worships a god of Moloch-attributes—and so on, beginning with the myth of Adam and Eve and crowning all with the millennium.

While he was on the subject of fundamentalism, I referred to the late William Jennings Bryan's assumed leadership of this systematized assault upon intelligence. He quoted in reply the following from his *Science and Civilization:*

> Mr. Bryan was an honored friend of mine, yet this need not prevent the observation that the skull with which Nature endowed him visibly approached the Neanderthal type. Feelings and the use of gesticulations and words are more according to the nature of this type than investigations and reflection. Those who would legislate against the teaching of evolution should also legislate against gravity, electricity and the unreasonable velocity of light, and also should introduce a clause to prevent the use of the telescope, the microscope and the spectroscope, or any other instrument of precision which may in the future be invented, constructed or used for the discovery of truth.

He noticed in this mass of correspondence that the tone of the writers who defended fundamentalism was the essence of cocksureness. Many had written as if they were private secretaries to Jehovah. It would not be possible to overestimate the injury to truth resulting from their arrogant and bigoted stand against the facts demonstrated by the progress of science. He was reminded of the saying of Oliver Wendell Holmes, who said that "the bigot is like the pupil of the eye—the more light you put upon it the more it will contract."

I emphasized the widespread revolt of the young, intelligent minds of our country against the demand, in the face of the revelation of science, for unconditional surrender made upon them in the name of blind faith. My ministry, which has dealt largely with young men, had convinced me that the bulk of the thoughtful ones are adrift. They rebel against this organized assault upon their intelligence. Just as soon as their studies reach the point that their childhood faith is shattered and they become convinced that they have been duped, that fable and fact have been jumbled together in their early instruction, they drop out in disgust. Hundreds come to me, in their distress, asking for help. The situation is heartbreaking. I was convinced that the story of his early experiences and an account of his final ransom from the shackles of superstition would be of priceless value to them—a source of strength and hope.

Burbank admitted this wholesale withdrawal of intelligent young men and young women from structural religion. It was the logical—the inevitable—

step. To have been able to help them would have been the joy of his life. If he found it necessary more than fifty years ago to take that stand to retain his self-respect, how much more urgent that necessity is in this day of illuminating spiritual power and accurate scientific research.

His early religious training was the product of the false teaching of the day, typical of the New England religion of the "sixties." As a young member of the Baptist Church of Lancaster, Massachusetts, his mind was filled with images of a God that made this world a dark, forbidding dwelling place. At a time when religion, which is a sentiment, should have developed in him a personality of trustful love, God was pictured as a being of severe, cruel attributes, a stern judge with the advocate, Jesus, staying the avenging hand. Fear was used like the lash of a slave-owner to force people to "Christian living." A hell of eternal torment was pictured before his young mind. The devil was imaged, in the language of Peter, to be the dread adversary, a "roaring lion," walking about seeking whom he might devour. Human conduct was fashioned on the doctrine of rewards and punishments. The message of hope might be summed up in the words, "He that believeth not shall be damned." As he was conceived and born in sin, the creature of total depravity, he was encouraged to look upon himself as a worm of the dust. It was a religion of cold, conventional, unloving, selfish spirit. Often his mind revolted, in its agony of doubt and distrust, for the entire system appealed to him as an outrage upon his youth and an absolute falsifying of life-values.

The one redeeming fact in those days of fog was the
loving, fostering care of his mother, whose spirit
revolted against the puritanic gloom that surrounded
them and permitted him to see another life unfolded
to him by her love. In his seventeenth year came the
first great awakening. Rambling one day in the woods,
his thoughts were centered on the beautiful things
of Nature, abounding on every hand, and the Infinite
Creative Power behind all. As he drank in the beauty
of form and color and fragrance, his mind caught a
vision of the Infinite Being that was in harmony with
the things he beheld in the realm of Nature. Then
there came an ugly, dark cloud that caused the vision
to vanish. It was that cruel, unloving, avenging God
of his church, a thing of awful ugliness. It was all so
hideous, so unreal to his young mind that he rose
from the ground, as if to cast it from him. And when
the cloud disappeared there came another vision
infinitely clearer. He beheld God in the flowers and
in the trees of the forest, in the purple hills beyond.
He was revealed as the true, the only infinite Creative
Force, and as he beheld him so a flood of light came
into his being and an overwhelming joy ineffable possessed him. Surely, "The invisible things of him from
the creation of the world are clearly seen, being understood by the things that are made." The bare thought
of having such a being imaged before his mind any
longer in terms of unloveliness, of accursed superstitions, of hatred and revenge, caused him to fling the
lying deception from him.

It was the God of love, the God of science that was
opened out invitingly to his young mind. And the

cruelty, the baseness of defaming such a Being in the
falsehoods of a religious system filled him with shame
and horror. Then it was that he made up his mind
to smash the chains of superstition that bound him,
and assert his freedom from the tyranny of tradition.
A conscious cosmic power possessed him, leaving the
deepest and most abiding impression on his young
life. From that hour, the church had lost its power
over him, and it was lost forever. Sixty years have
passed—years that demanded from him the closest,
most patient investigation in the path of science.
These experiences were a power in working out his
philosophy of life. And the closer he was carried into
the secrets of Nature, the nearer he found himself
to the great, almighty Force. He never failed him.
The spirit of life, sunlight and truth crushed within
him the spirit of darkness, superstition and death. It
was his belief that the God within us is the only
available God we know, or can know, and the clear
light of science teaches us that we must be our own
saviors, if we are to be found worth saving; in other
words, we must depend upon the "Kingdom within."

What an experience! What a glorious ransom from
spiritual bondage! And yet thousands on thousands
of young men and women are to-day passing through
the same experience. We were taught in the "eighties"
just what he was taught in the "sixties." When I was
an undergraduate in dear old Trinity College, Dublin,
I was in contact with hundreds of young men who
yearned for a like freedom. We were bound in chains
mightier far in Ireland than those he endured in New
England. Our university professors chafed under the

dogmatism thrust upon them. The pulpit of our
college chapel was denied John Pentland Mahaffy,
our ablest scholar, for daring to question certain theological drivel. Professor Lee was threatened with a
heresy trial for denying the verbal inspiration of the
Bible. One day, in our Greek class, Mahaffy turned
from his "Homer" to answer the question of a student
on a matter of ethics, and the talk switched into
religion. Finally he said: "It may not be in my day;
but you, young gentlemen, will live to see a new
religion—a religion molded by scholarship and science,
and that day will spell 'doom' for structural theology."
It sounded like a confirmation of Canon Farrar, of the
Church of England, who said: "Science has had a
struggle for life against the fury of theological dogmatists, but in every instance the dogmatists have
been ignominiously defeated."

Burbank was convinced that day is now here. It
was the dream of his life—his constant hope—that we
might live to see the RELIGION OF HUMANITY. Yes! it
is now here, he said. He meant the religion of sympathy, kindness, love, peace, harmony and health. It
is the spirit of life, soul-light, not darkness, superstition and *death*. Science, he went on, has shown us all
that we know about what we call God—there is no
other real knowledge besides; all else is without a
shadow of proof for those who think. As he looked
back upon the events of the last quarter of a century,
he could trace its gradual approach and unfolding. A
new spirit had come into the world, as the evolution
of science. Error is giving way to truth, as evil does

when overcome with good. There was first needed a tearing down, before the building up. And the wreckers of the old musty beliefs and superstitions are a preparatory part of the very structure. As John Fiske said: "One and all the orthodox creeds are crumbling into ruins everywhere. We now witness the constructive work on a foundation that will endure through the ages. That foundation is the god of science—revealed to us in terms that will harmonize with our intelligence."

The world, he said, is sure to welcome with intense interest this conception of the basic principles of the Religion of Humanity. Millions of men and women in this country, and beyond the seas, are ready for it. How the writers of those thousands of letters appeal for more light and the expression for their benefit of a reasonable faith and hope!

The Religion of Humanity, Burbank felt, will be founded on belief in one Eternal Energy—almighty and omnipresent. This universe without a God was incredible to him. Huxley never wrote anything more logical, in his judgment, than this:

I am utterly unable to conceive the existence of matter, if there is no mind to feature that existence. The problem of the ultimate cause of existence is one which seems to me hopelessly out of reach of my poor powers. Of all the senseless babble, the demonstrations of these philosophers who undertake to tell us all about the nature of God would be the worst, if they were

not surpassed by the still greater absurdities of
the philosophers who try to prove that there is
no God.

In reading this statement to me, Burbank accentuated the words: *"If they were not surpassed by the
still greater absurdities of the philosophers who try
to prove that there is no God."* Take Buddhism, for
example, he exclaimed. While his teaching seemed
to eliminate the idea of a god, his followers, finding
it necessary to worship some god, made a god of
Buddha. This same thing befell the teaching of Zara-
thustra in ancient Persia. Religion cannot be founded
on a principle; it needs the power of an Eternal
Energy, almighty and omnipresent. Burbank had
already made that point clear when he said: "I prefer
and claim the right to worship the infinite, everlasting,
almighty God of this vast universe as revealed to
us gradually, step by step, by the demonstrable truths
of our savior, science."

Yet, in the face of that statement, hundreds
denounced him by letter—as an "atheist." It is true
he was an atheist in his utter denial of the God of
the theologians, but that denial makes his faith all
the stronger in the God of science.

One Eternal Energy! One Infinite Spirit! There
will you find the foundation of his faith, the one
Supreme Source of the philosophy of his life. And this
Infinite Energy is the very life of the world, the inspiration of all things created. It is the idea of God, as
revealed to us from the "Kingdom within." God is
immanent, Burbank believed. "In Him we live, and

move, and have our being." This Infinite Spirit was to him not a personality living in a distant realm, enthroned like a king, dispensing His authority. He is a part of everything created. He is in the plants, in the flowers, in the stars, in the worlds beyond. He is the one, supreme, in-dwelling God in our lives. With this Being it was Burbank's delight to live for sixty years, in the beauty and silences of Nature. His immanence was so real to him that he beheld Him in the living things of Nature that passed through his hands. And for him, this revelation of the "Kingdom within" destroyed all false conceptions of God.

The old Hebrew, anthropomorphic conception of the Deity, he believed, is disappearing, forced out by an intelligence that brands it puerile and absurd. Man-made gods, as all religions indicate, were imaged in the likeness of man. His human virtues and his vices have been magnified in the nature of the gods. Revenge, jealousy and all the dark passions have been given recognition, side by side, with all the manly virtues. In this way we can understand the Buddha of the Chinese, the Jehovah of the Hebrews, the Ormuzd and Ahriman of the Persians, the Osiris of the Egyptians, the Teutates of the Gauls, the Jupiter of the Greeks, the great Allah of the Mussulman. Each age had its own god, who rose in quality in man's conception with the steps of advance of successive ages. God has been represented in the capacity of King, Man of War, Judge and Merciless Avenger, ruling his subjects with an arbitrary spirit. To this method of god-making, and the tendency of mankind to cling to the ruder conceptions, we owe, he maintained, the horrors of war, perpetuated through the ages.

Burbank was conscious that those dark ages possessed the beautiful sentiments of the Twenty-third Psalm and the rapturous music of the great poet Isaiah! He was cognizant that even the darkest ages have given to the world fragments of the richness of that "Kingdom within," which rose high above the savagery and crudeness abounding on every hand. But, he said, we know that those ages were influenced for evil by the falseness of the gods thus created. Following are the words, from the pen of Camille Flammarion, taken from his *Dreams of an Astronomer,* to which Burbank once invited me to listen:

> The search for the nature of the First Cause— I do not say "the knowledge of God" which would be an expression worthy a "theologian" and absurd in itself—but simply the search for the absolute Being, for the origin of the energy which sustains, animates and governs the universe, for the intelligent force which acts everywhere and perpetually through infinity and eternity, and gives rise to the appearances which strike our eyes and are studied by our science—this search, I say—could not be undertaken nor even properly conceived before the first discoveries of astronomy and modern physics. Man has conceived a God in his own likeness. It is in the name of this pretended God that monarchs and pontiffs have in all the ages, and under cover of all religions, bound humanity in a slavery from which it has not yet freed itself. It is in the

name of this God who "protects Germany," "protects England," "protects France," "protects Russia," "protects Turkey," protects all the divisions
and all the barbarities, that even in our own day
the so-called civilized people of our planet have
been armed in war against each other; like mad
dogs have hurled themselves upon one another
in a conflict over which falsehood and hypocrisy,
seated on the steps of the thrones, figure a "God
of Armies" as presiding, a God who blesses the
daggers and plunges his hands in the smoking
blood of victims to mark the forehead of kings.
It is to this God that altars are raised and *Te
Deums* are chanted. It is in the names of the
gods of Olympus that the Greeks condemned
Socrates to drink the hemlock; it is in the name
of Jehovah that the high-priests and Pharisees
crucified Jesus. It is in the name of Jesus, himself become God, that fanaticism ignominiously
condemned to the stake men like Giordano Bruno,
Vanini, Etienne Dolet, John Huss, Savonarola,
and numerous other heroic victims; that the
Inquisition ordered Galileo to belie his conscience;
that thousands and thousands of unfortunates
accused of witchcraft were burnt alive in popular
ceremonies; it was with the express benediction
of Pope Gregory the Thirteenth that the butchery
of St. Bartholomew drenched Paris in blood.

"Strong words of a great scientist, built on facts!"
Burbank exclaimed.

He felt that to the Hebrews goes the credit of
inventing the conception of our monotheistic Jewish-

Christian God, who, however, is represented to be jealous, cruel, vindictive, and to possess most of the weaknesses and bad habits of primitive man. When Robert Ingersoll had the courage to flout the idea of such a God, he was branded a hardened atheist by the theological dogmatists. What he did believe may be understood, in Burbank's estimation, from one of his last utterances: "I belong to the great church that holds the world within its starlit aisles; that claims the great and the good of every race and clime; that finds with joy the grain of gold in every creed, and floods with light and love the germs of good in every soul."

Over the entrance of such a church, Burbank said, and it will appeal to vast millions, may be written the name of the God of science.

He was sure that man, as time goes on, will picture in his soul God the spirit whose moral attributes transcend to infinity his own highest ideals of goodness. He will image the Spirit of Light and Love and Truth —an all-loving Being so close to the poorest of his creatures that no go-between is needed. And as the "Kingdom within" develops those moral attributes, it will reveal glimpses into new depths of the eternal qualities of love, of mercy, of kindness, of peace, of harmony and health.

For fifty years and more Burbank had lived and toiled in the deep silences of Nature, amid the lives of plants and flowers, and had experienced a small share of what such a Being may be to the sons of men. Such an Omnipresence needed for him no local habitation, no magic of sacrament, wherein to reveal himself. His presence permeates all. Under Jewish teaching, where racial religion was supreme, there was a "Holy of Holies." But in the words of Jesus: "Neither in this mountain, nor in Jerusalem, shall ye worship the Father. . . . God is a Spirit, and they that worship him must worship him in spirit and in truth."

Toward this broader vision of the Eternal Spirit he was confident the world is fast moving. It has taken centuries to develop. Every new triumph in the world of science has hastened the day. The barriers of man-made creeds will be swept aside as unworthy and untrue expressions of His Being. The narrowness of sects, warring one against the other, will be lost in the revelation of one almighty God dwelling in every creature. This comprehensive ideal will gather within its folds the Universal Father, the biological conception of a vital force, pervading the universe.

This is all expressed in the sayings of the world's greatest Teacher, of whom Burbank began to talk in this wise. Jesus stands out, in bold relief, as greatest amongst the sons of men. The human, historic Jesus is the supreme fact of all time. This both Jews and Gentiles alike acknowledge, he declared, and the strong position concerning him taken recently by Rabbi Stephen Wise in New York is bold, logical and conclusive. Jesus was our world's greatest teacher. Buddha left many important truths, as did Mohammed and Confucius; but they cannot compare with the truths that were taught by the humble Nazarene. Notwithstanding our altered civilization, our advance in science and social betterment, his teaching is as real and natural to our spiritual discernment to-day as it was when he spoke to that small group of unlearned and illiterate men and women by the sea of Galilee. That fact alone would place him first amongst the teachers of the world. Truth alone stands the test of time. Truth alone may be applied to all ages and conditions. Jesus was an idealist, he reminded me, and his rules of daily living must always be analyzed with this fact in mind. Men may mock at the impracticable nature of his teachings, as an impossible code to regulate the world of business, of society, of morals; or they may brand him as "out of date." But they mock because they want to change his teaching to suit their mode of living, rather than to change their mode of living to conform with his teaching. Truth was imaged on the camera of his mind with a clearness and finality unique amongst men.

That explained, in Burbank's judgment, the revolt of all forms of error and falsehood. Jesus came "not to destroy, but to fulfil." He found that the Jewish religion had lost its vital spark. All kinds of superstition, peculiar to dark ages, had so distorted the message of the Jehovah that noonday was turned into night. And as a logical result, his generation became creatures of the letter that killeth, and lost the spirit that giveth life. Their desecration of the Temple typified their utter callousness. As a Jew, his young life was wholly given up to a merciless exposure of the rottenness of their system of belief. To Burbank, his denunciation of the Scribes and Pharisees is the severest arraignment of error and hypocrisy in all history. Jesus was the infidel of his day and generation. With petrified hypocrites thirsting for his blood, Calvary was his inevitable goal, so far was he in advance of

his time. Nothing in history equals the spirit of
hatred, of bitter enmity that sent him to his death.
Passion so blinded men that they could see in him
no beauty of character. His hatred of organized falsehood was only equaled by his love of unspoiled humanity. No man ever lived who uttered his message with
such naturalness and simplicity. Jesus, of all great
teachers, claimed least for self. Of no one were greater
claims falsely made. His humanness is the jewel of
his soul. He lived a life of poverty, of self-abnegation,
of a vagabond, for "he had not where to lay his head."
He was the friend of publicans and of sinners. He
saw in every man and every woman the best and the
noblest, and inspired them with hope and courage.
His love for little children, for the poor and the
oppressed, for the earnest seeker after truth is unparal-
leled in history. His psychical powers were beyond
the range of calculation. Had he been interpreted
through the ages just as he was, his life amongst men
would harmonize with the truths of advanced science.

The man Jesus lived, Burbank went on, the most
beautiful life in history. The God Jesus, as developed
in subsequent ages by man-made creeds, he said, is a
distortion of the truth of that life. Structural theology
has built up an entirely false interpretation of his
being. Burbank had no hesitation in asserting that the
Christianity of the twentieth century, as framed by
theological dogmatists, is absolutely different from the
simple, direct truths taught by Jesus. His humanity
is merged in doctrines of deification. He who rebuked
a certain ruler for addressing him as "Good Master,"
and added, "Why callest thou me good? there is none

good but one, that is, God," is now called "Very God of very God, begotten not made, being of one substance with the Father." If he were alive in human flesh to-day, how he would rebuke those makers of idols! All this is a relic of polytheism.

Burbank loved to think of him as the babe of Bethlehem, the child of Nazareth, the son of the carpenter, the friend of man, the son of God, whose love, gentleness, patience, mercy and spirit of self-sacrifice make him divine. His reverence and love toward him were too great to worship him. His incarnation is turned into mist by the doctrine of the virgin birth, he maintained. His ministry has been clouded with the miraculous. Angels and demons have been invented to hover around his person. We lose sight of the human Jesus in the aureole of Deity created by simple-minded followers, magnified by theologians and colored by artists and poets through the centuries. His personality is lost in the confusion of metaphysics. This will account for the story of his bodily resurrection, and his ascension, in bodily form, to take his place at the right hand of the throne of God. This false conception of the son of God is the essence of anthropomorphism.

In contrast, the Christ of science will be a potent force, he predicted, in the Religion of Humanity. He will be reverenced as first of all the great teachers of the world. He will be interpreted as he lived and died amongst men. He will be the greatest personality of all time in pointing out to man the "Kingdom within." This is what Burbank meant when he said in his address: "We must not be deceived by blind leaders of the blind, calmly expecting to be 'saved' by any one except by the Kingdom within ourselves. The truly honest and brave ones know that if saved it must be by their own efforts." Amongst the new cults in organized rebellion against the false conceptions of the Jesus of the gospel we find Christian Science. The accession to that cult of so many Jews seemed to him an indication of the yearning for a reasonable basis of belief in the ranks of Judaism.

He foretold that millions would hail as reasonable this attitude in relation to the God whom we love to call Infinite Spirit. With this monotheistic foundation this Religion of Humanity will re-interpret the Bible on a basis that will make a similar appeal of reasonableness to men with a modern training, he declared. The New Religion will interpret the Bible in the light of modern science and scholarship.

As Burbank in his address in San Francisco made clear, the Bible should be treated with everyday common sense. "Let us read the Bible," he then said, "without the ill-fitting colored spectacles of theology, just as we read other books, using our own judgment and reason, listening to the voice within, not to the noisy babble without." Strange to say, in religion only have men persisted in defending exploded theories. In every branch of science, when facts are revealed that oppose long-established beliefs, the old error has to give way to new truth. It was so in the science of medicine on the discovery of the circulation disease was radically altered. No medical scientist of the blood by Dr. Harvey, when the treatment of could cling to the old and retain his place as a physician. It was true of astronomy when the discovery of

Galileo swept away the false systems relating to the universe. It is so in every scientific study.

Burbank was compelled, during his fifty years of research, to reject many an error in the treatment of plant life, and his success was largely due, he felt, to his intuitive insistence in rejecting the false and applying the true. Science and the God of science are one. Religion and science owe their life to the same Source. No one can hope to stop the progress of science any more than he can the progress of the suns and the stars in their courses. Yet when we turn to religion we find a mode of operation in fashion destructive to the truth. Men of reputed intelligence insist on clinging to falsehood, in spite of the positive demonstration of science to the contrary and the veto pronounced by the critical research of scholarship.

Take, for example, he said, the story of creation as contained in the book of Genesis. No scientist would dare to endorse it as a fact in history. It belongs in the long list of myths abounding in those books supposed to have been written by Moses. Yet men have the audacity to face audiences of recognized mentality with the blatant affirmation that it is one of the great facts of history. Errors of text, errors of incident, errors of numerals are constantly to be found throughout the books that compose the Bible. Fact and fable are mixed together in bewildering confusion. Poetry and prose are interpreted as of equal historical value. A satanic devil is clothed with a personality expressed in terms as clearly defined as that of almighty God. Yet in the face of this all too patent situation, those men, whose vocation implies an intelligent knowledge of the Bible, cling to the doctrine of verbal inspiration with the vain notion that the integrity of "the word of God" must be conserved, even by believing an untruth. This is an assault, he maintained, upon intelligence. It is the continued application of medieval methods in an age of enlightenment.

Thus may we account for the present tottering state of structural religion. It is inevitable that every false claim which the student detects weakens his faith in the integrity of the Bible. And it likewise weakens his faith in the integrity of that interpreter. He reasons that the man, in spite of his profession that he has been "divinely called," is either grossly ignorant or wilfully misleading. If the false claims advanced by him are the result of ignorance, his right to stand in the pulpit is questionable; if, on the other hand, he knowingly insists that falsehood is truth, the integrity of his character is shaken.

If the Religion of Humanity may hope to restore the faith of the millions who have rejected structural theology, Burbank once said, the Bible will be accepted as a *part* revelation of the God of science. Its influence through the centuries has been felt in the heart of all nations. It has been translated into every language, and its teachings have molded countless millions of lives in nobleness of character. Of all books it is the most sacred and the most precious. We call it a book, whereas it is a series of revelations from the crudest ages to the second century of the Christian era. Its circulation throughout the world is equal to that of all other books combined. And as the ages roll on, it will continue to be a mighty force in shaping the

destiny of men and of nations. No literature in the
world of letters can compare with it. You will search
in vain, he told me, for the poet who can surpass the
Prophet Isaiah. His thoughts have risen to heights
beyond human imagination. The simple beauty of
the sayings of Jesus transcends anything in the world's
religions. But the Bible is only one of the varied
ways in which the Spirit of the Infinite is made
known. He has revealed himself through Confucius,
Mohammed, Buddha and other great leaders, whose
writings have influenced, and still influence, millions
of lives. In revelation, as in all things, the law of
evolution has been at work. Ideas have been transplanted from the soil of one religion to that of another,
without an effort to link the sources. Quoting a well-
known scholar, he said: "There is hardly a great or
fruitful idea in the Jewish or Christian system which
has not its analogy in the ancient Egyptian faith."
Out of systems of religion that our so-called Christian civilization calls "pagan" have been evolved
truths that taught men how to live the noblest type
of life.

The Religion of Humanity, he predicted, will extend
a welcome to the religions of the world whose teachings have inspired men to deeds of love, of mercy, of
service to their fellows. In the light of these facts,
we must share with them the duty of a world salvation. It was a Christian scholar, he cautioned me, who
admitted that "Moslem morality is better than our
own. Islam has abolished drunkenness, gambling and
prostitution—the three curses of Christian lands."
Revelation is not static; it is progressive. Yet theo-

logians will insist in claiming that the Bible is a "final"
revelation.   Upon whose authority was the canon of
Scripture closed?   Burbank quoted in this connection
his position as set forth in his address: "I prefer and
claim the right to worship the infinite, everlasting,
almighty God of this vast universe as revealed to us
gradually, step by step, by the demonstrable truths of
our savior, science."   He is revealed in our own day
with a power greater than that shown in the past, for
the reason that such revelation is made by the simplicity of science, not by the illusion of miracle.
Every fresh conquest in the sphere of science, especially those that add to the sum of human happiness,
is a revelation confirming the love and almightiness of
God.   He is revealed in the modern discoveries of
science that have prolonged human life, lessened
human pain and conquered disease.   We have con-
cluded the first quarter of our century with a record
of revelations unique in the history of the world.   We
now stand in the dawn of a radiant morn that promises
a flood of light from truth unfolded by the critical
work of scholarship and the fresh discoveries of science.   And the second quarter of our century, he ven-
tured to predict, will see a still greater revelation.
That precious Book, preserved through the mist of
ages, will be interpreted in the light of the law that
controls the literature of the world.   It will reveal
the God of science, stripped of the superstitions that
have made His name grotesque, and present a version
of His character acceptable to an age of enlightenment.
It will dispel the magic of miracle and express the
almightiness of the Infinite Spirit in terms of natural

law. Sacraments of miraculous conceit will be interpreted in their true spirit. Dogmatic arrogancy will
give way to the right of individual variation in belief.
And when that Book is truly understood we are bound
to learn, he emphasized, that religion is as natural to
man and as important to each human being and to
the welfare of society as breathing, but, like love, it
cannot be fully described by any single fact. It is
justice, love, truth, peace and harmony combined—a
serene unity at peace with science and the laws of
the universe. The religion of science, ethics, service,
and of love and good will is not indissolubly connected
with obsolete misleading theologies, which bear the
same relation to the essence of true religion that scar-
let fever, mumps and measles do to education. Even
men to-day are far from free. They are still slaves
to war, crime, bigotry and ignorance—the only "unpardonable sin"; slaves to unnumbered ancient taboos,
superstitions, prejudices and fallacies. But one by one
these are slowly and surely weakening under the clear
light of the morning of science, the savior of mankind.
Science, which has opened our eyes to the vastness
of the universe, has replaced darkness, ignorance, bigotry and superstition with light, truth and freedom
from fear. Such is the picture he drew of a world in
which the true Savior has been revealed.

On the subject of prayer, Burbank was equally illuminating. To him prayer was truly the life of religion.
But the entire conception of prayer, he said, has been
perverted by false, superstitious ideas concerning an
omnipresent God. The reality of prayer depends upon
a truer conception of the Being with whom communion

is sought. One needs only to think of the many false ways in which such a God is interpreted. He is pictured as Ruler of the universe, enthroned in heavenly habitation, dispensing His will as in the early days of the Hebrew people. He is the "God of Armies." As such in great crises is he approached and his aid invoked. Thus, during the World War, ending in November of 1918, in which the Christian nations combined to kill off ten million lives of the flower of the world's manhood, each nation petitioned this "God of Armies" to direct the instruments of death to its victory and His eternal glory. No war in history was waged with more diabolical cruelty. No tortures in the darkest ages of heathendom could compare with the fiendishness of the weapons employed and the awful human destruction involved. Every victory, with blood-lust fierce as the tiger, was hailed with national thanksgiving and accepted as direct answer to the suppliant cries of the people.

He is pictured as the anthropomorphic God, the superman, who once "walked in the garden in the cool of the day"; with long, flowing beard, like Michelangelo's God in the Sistine Chapel; or like Otricoli's Roman Jupiter in the Vatican, cringing beggars kneeling before him, craving every form of temporal gift. Millions of such petitions, including favors as numerous as the stars, are uttered at the same moment of time.

He is pictured as the God of theology, who presides over a world into which every child that is born is the "child of wrath," demanding the cleansing power of rite or sacrament to save its life from eternal

destruction. Conceived and born in sin and pre-
damned at birth! And this same God is petitioned to
release from the burning torments of hell, in response
to the appeals of the "faithful," those who have been
there consigned.

Such horrible conceptions of God, he believed, make
communion between the finite and the Infinite impossible. Prayers to such a Deity may float on the
incensed air in tones of celestial music or in the minor
chanting of long-drawn-out litanies, but they reach
only the prescribed area that scientifically regulates
the limit of sound. That there has been a revolt
against those perverted ideas of God is everywhere
apparent. No far-off Ruler, enthroned in majesty and
splendor, no anthropomorphic God, clothed in the gar-
ment of man's imagination, no cruel monster, whose
purpose in creation is fulfilled in destruction, no vindictive God, who takes pleasure in human misery, will
satisfy men to-day. Those false conceptions of the
Deity are doomed in the light of science. Prayer has
become a lost force in the world, not because man
does not feel its need, but simply because he prefers
to retain his manhood by refusal to treat with such
a God. Many of the most uncompromising atheists
in the religion of theology are ardent theists in the
religion of science.

The Religion of Humanity, he thought, will reveal
a God within us as the only companionable God we
can know. " 'Tis life and more of life we want." Life
as we see it around us on this planet is usually thought
to be confined to man, animals and plants, those
organisms which grow and reproduce their kind with

more or less precision. "Why should we omit crystals, which grow as truly as plants and reproduce themselves quite as precisely true to type, or the more primitive forms of life which are reproduced by division? Science is proving that the world is not half dead, but that every atom is all life and motion," were his words.

Now, as the God of science reveals Himself, we become conscious of a greater, stronger, more abundant life, of a spiritual universe filled with an all-loving, Spiritual Energy. This spiritual universe is the substantial, the real, for it nurtures our ideas, our aspirations.

Burbank often said to me that as he wandered amongst his plants and flowers and watched the gradual unfolding of Nature, his mind entered into cosmic communion with this inner, spiritual world, of which Nature is but a passing symbol. And in his cosmic consciousness, he said, God was within. He manifested Himself within him, around him. He was a conscious part of him. Infinitely beyond the power of demonstration, He was so real that self was lost in Him. The God of science is, therefore, all in all, he believed. If this were a mere passing experience, he said, a transient thrill of ecstasy, it would leave behind the suspicion that it might be only a piece of abnormal expression. But for fifty years and over he felt the abiding consciousness of this fellowship, intensified, as he believed, by the closeness of his life to Nature. And this uninterrupted fellowship revealed not only the God of science, but the law of the spiritual universe. As the result of over fifty years spent in the handling of plants, he had been amazed at the accuracy of natural law. He never found any calculation, basèd on the known laws of Nature, to err. Millions on millions of plants passed through his hands and he was struck by this precision. He had never been disappointed. He was convinced that the same Spiritual Enegry is controlling the spiritual universe. It is natural law in the spiritual world. Nothing is haphazard. There is no such thing as blind force. One sublime order pervades this unseen universe, with the almighty God within and behind all. It is not a God from the outside, as he explained it, drawn toward him by the appeal of his inner being, but rather the God rising within him, producing an overwhelming consciousness of the Infinite. In the conscious presence of this Power will be found the sources of the religious life. It cultivates, as nothing else can, the sentiment of awe and reverence, the love of goodness and beauty, all the tender pure passions of Nature. In the failure to grasp this truth may be found the prevailing perversion of prayer.

Is it strange, then, that prayer should have appealed to him as a force, absolutely independent of the human voice? To the omnipresent Spirit the only language that is real is the language of action. Because such a Being is approachable and this mode of approach is as natural as the attitude of a child toward its mother, the Religion of Humanity will appeal to intelligence. And therein lies the sole basis of happiness. It is enough to know that man's life, man's sphere, man's destiny are in the keeping of such a Power He was sure that no human relation could ever draw

the lives of earnest men and women into a bond so
sacred and serene. It brings effort and action, peace
and helpfulness.

The consciousness of such a bond impels the mind
of reason to revolt against the degraded habits of
prayer so common in structural religion. Noisy beggars, he called them, with clamorous petitions, address
themselves to the Deity with an air of vulgar assurance. They utter words, words, words, with a "Coué"
contempt for meaning and purpose, believing "they
will be heard for their much speaking." For such a
spirit of a mutilated religion did the prophet of old
express his contempt, when he mocked the prophets
of Baal and said: "Cry aloud: for he is a god; either
he is talking, or he is pursuing, or he is in a journey,
or peradventure he sleepeth, and must be awaked."
Men who thus interpret the omnipresent God miss
the source of truth. And the loss is beyond calculation. Scientifically accepted, he believed, there are
hidden powers capable of being developed in this
spiritual fellowship that surpass the comprehension of
mind. They account for the force of personality, of
self-control, of renewed strength, of the great love
toward our fellow man expressed in the joy of service
for their good, for the calm assurance that this omnipresent God is all-love and all-truth. A terrible load
of responsibility rests upon the heads of those who
hold earnest lives back from the supreme privilege of
communing with God by presenting to them distorted
Deities before whom they refuse to kneel.

Burbank was a sincere admirer of George Eliot, and
once read to me a letter written by her to Harriet

Beecher Stowe, dated May 6, 1869, which gives expression to these sentiments:

> I believe that religion has to be modified—"developed," according to the dominant phrase—and that a religion more perfect than any yet prevalent must express less care for personal consolation, and a more deeply awing sense of responsibility to man, springing from sympathy with that which of all things is most certainly known to us, the difficulty of the human lot. I do not find my temple in Pantheism, which, whatever might be its value speculatively, could not yield a practical religion, since it is an attempt to look at the universe from the outside of our relations to it [that universe] as human beings. As healthy, sane human beings, we must love and hate—love what is good for mankind, hate what is evil for mankind.

Here now we come, he commented, to the great dividing line that separates the old from the new religion. With her keen spiritual insight and high moral courage, George Eliot expresses it in matchless form: "A religion more perfect than any yet prevalent must express less care for personal consolation, and a more deeply awing sense of responsibility to man, springing from sympathy with that which of all things is most certainly known to us, the difficulty of the human lot." He tried to give utterance to much the same thought in his address in San Francisco: "Let us have one world at a time and let us make the journey one of joy to our fellow passengers and just as convenient and happy for them as we can, and trust the rest as we trust life."

Institutional religion is divided, it seemed to him, in interest between two worlds, with over-attention to the hereafter. As David Starr Jordan well said: "To live in two worlds at once is to unfit oneself for life in any world." It is true that in proportion as men have dwelt in the hereafter they have neglected the here-and-now. It is simply impossible that people should be absorbingly interested in a personal and selfish fashion in the hereafter, and at the same time be interested, in a noble and humane way, in the life that now is. This is seen in the effect which this attitude produced upon the lives of the first disciples in the Christian faith. Their intense interest in the future life caused them to be indifferent to the present and made of them poor citizens. How could it be otherwise? They looked for a hasty and sudden end during their lifetime to things earthly, and their absorption in what they called the "second coming" left them no inspiration to better human conditions. Paul was compelled to write to one church to calm the fears of the disciples over the expected cataclysm and to assure them there was no immediate danger. These early Christians had a magnified self-interest in the future life. Present conditions were lost sight of in the attention given to future glory or punishment. Religious revivals in days past reflect this same attitude. Preachers played on the emotion of their hearers by painting a fantastic heaven with the brush of Swedenborg, and a hell with the carmine of Dante.

On the other hand, he thought that there had been

a complete reversal in recent decades in the human outlook upon life. No longer is man thrilled by the rapturous vision of a future heaven nor terrified by the dread descriptions of a future hell. Both have had their day—creations of dark, noisome superstition. In the light of science the glorious present is all important; the Oriental imagery of the future belongs to fable. Heaven and hell are here and now. As Milton said: "The mind is its own place and in itself can make a heaven of hell, a hell of heaven." "Let us have one world at a time." In the face of a structural religion that brings to mind empty churches and tens of millions of men and women who have no desire for it, there is a challenge going forth from the Religion of Humanity that will meet with a universal response. It will evoke that response because it will appeal to the noblest, the best that is in them. It will see in all men some good—the real—capable of being developed to unlimited power. It will fit men and women for their true place in life and never fail to give the helping hand. It was this thought, he felt, that captured the imagination of George Eliot and filled her mind with a new vision. To see in all men some good means that the inspiration has been found to help them.

With his plants, Luther Burbank always started with sound, wholesome life and worked upon that as a sure foundation. Theology starts out wrong. To brand an innocent babe born into this world without its own volition as the child of wrath and, as it grows into maturity, to add the damnable doctrine of total depravity is an awful crime against humanity. If he dared to treat his plants as religionists treat the moral being, he said, he would have been the greatest failure in the long list of scientists. It would be like casting a blight upon their young plant lives before the first experiment was tried. Human plants are more sensitive and respond even more rapidly to proper treatment. A religion founded on an abiding faith in the love of the everlasting God of this universe is the great need of humanity. This will be the supreme test. "Pure religion and undefiled" applies a spark to our better impulses, and directs their forces into channels of human betterment.

Fired by the consciousness of man's true place in the world and directed for his good, the New Religion will summon into active play great stores of human energies now latent. Glittering generalities will give place to personal forces hard at work. The words "service for others," for example, will acquire a new meaning. Love will be its inspiring power and unselfishness its very soul. During the past fifty years, the greatest movements for the uplift of humanity have sprung from sources outside the churches. Religion, as interpreted by our race, has developed the sentiment of self-interest. Men are asked to choose between the alternatives offered by a God with heaven in the one hand and hell in the other. With such a God the average man of self-respect wants to have nothing to do. No religion based on selfishness can survive. Pure religion consists of active philanthropy and personal holiness. Religion is real when man, under the power of its influence, loses himself in the good of his fellow man. That was the secret in the life of the man of Galilee, who "went about doing good." Renunciation was the law of Christ. If men would dwell less on the miracles which an age of magic attributed to Jesus and dwell more on that greatest of all miracles, his life of absolute self-abnegation in an age of utter selfishness, his true place in the world would be restored.

The Religion of Humanity, Burbank predicted, will be a living challenge to do and to serve; man striving to help his fellow man, inspired by the thought of his greater welfare and happiness. Our world is undergoing a gradual preparation for the universal reception of such a religion. Herein science and religion are working together. Science, by reason of her modern discoveries, has made of this world one large family. Nations are like next-door neighbors. Our doings are flashed in a few seconds to the ends of the earth. Time and space have been annihilated by miracles of science, greater far than the age of magic and ignorance could have invented. Human knowledge has advanced with marvelous strides. The hundreds of millions who have turned from all structural religion, as commonly presented to them, are ready to examine a religion that may suggest a reasonable belief and hope. The state of moral and financial bankruptcy in which the nations of Europe emerged from the World War emphasized the need of spiritual realities. There was an absolute reversal of truth. Peace gave way to the sword, good will to hatred, spiritual ideals to material passions. We were taught our lesson, and the Religion of Humanity will establish personal service for others on the foundation of love. It has been a long step between the "traces of altruism appearing even in animals of a single cell" to the present spirit of altruism as exhibited between man and man.

Here, once more, science and religion are working in harmony. Modern miracles in the sphere of medical science, founded on reason, have surpassed the greatest miracles of theology, founded on fancy. Our century registers hundreds of such miracles, working for the good of humanity. Through their influence, suffering and pain are lessened, new hope is inspired and the measure and happiness of the human span of life increased. Think of the blessings, he said, bestowed upon humanity by the life-work of scientists, such as our Dr. Crawford Long, discoverer of ether, Koch of Germany, Lister of England, and Pasteur of France. Men and women of the type of Pierre and Madame Curie, who, after a life-consecration, gave to the world their discoveries of radium and polonium, are worthy of saintship in the Religion of Humanity. Think of the number of scientists who have willingly yielded their lives in experimental tests of new discoveries for the conquest of disease! If this spirit of altruism filled the world men would no longer speculate, but would know what is meant by "the new heaven and the new earth." Such a conception of service, applied with universal intentness, would turn this world from a desert into a garden. Nor must we forget, he cautioned, that we are only at the threshold of this new conception of service. It will not be long before the two great plagues of humanity, tuberculosis and cancer, with their excruciating suffering, are conquered by the researches of science. Miracles per-

formed by religionists of the first century are said to
have restored individuals to health. Miracles performed by scientists of the twentieth century restore
hundreds of thousands. Here may we find the source
of that richer, fuller, more abundant life that is the
essence of religion.

But, in some respects, greater than all in its promise
is that re-directed energy, in this life of service, now
being felt in the world. We are in a position to approach crime, poverty, ignorance and human misery
from a new angle. Religions of the past were directly
responsible for the false methods used in their day.
Whereas, through ignorance the supreme effort then
was to *cure,* from this day forward the supreme aim
will be to *prevent.* Under the past-and-gone system,
encouraged by theological falsehoods, the stages of a
criminal's career were marked by a dense stupidity
almost impossible to conceive. He was born the "child
of wrath" and neglected in his formative years of boyhood, thereby becoming the logical vehicle of crime
and the victim of the penitentiary. When he had
reached his cell he was so far recognized as to be
included in the prayers of "the faithful" who petitioned for his redemption. What can be expected
when two of the great Christian denominations say
that from birth he was "dead in sin, wholly defiled in
all the faculties and parts of soul and body, and
therefore bound over to the wrath of God"! The
blight which a false theology thus casts upon life is
destructive from the start. But such damnable errors
are being crushed.

Our New Religion, in his view, will enunciate the

non-reality of evil in comparison with the infinite reality of good. It will behold in the child the human plant that may bud and blossom in a garden teeming with the sanctity of life. Here, once more, will be found the harmonious working of science and religion, both making, like good partners, for the same results.

In Burbank's book, *Training of the Human Plant*, he said that all animal life is sensitive to environment, but of all living things the child is the most sensitive. Surroundings act upon it as the outside world acts upon the plate of the camera. Every possible influence to which it is subject will leave its impress upon the child, and in many cases the traits which it inherited will become to a certain extent even more pronounced than as given in heredity. The child is like a cut diamond, its many facets receiving sharp, clear impressions not possible to a pebble—with this difference, however, that the change wrought in the child from the influences without becomes constitutional and ingrained. A child absorbs environment. It is the most susceptible thing in the world to influence, and if that force be applied rightly and constantly when the child is in its most receptive condition, the effect will be pronounced, immediate and permanent. As science and religion combine to bring the law of prevention into the life of the young human plant, the new methods of service will be unfolded.

And love, he believed, will be the cornerstone of the temple. Burbank's whole philosophy of life was built on love as the foundation. It is the supreme force that puts man in tune with the Infinite, he said. No religion can survive without it. Creeds are cold, often

senseless, confessions of faith. Forms and ceremonies
are mere outer garments, too often falsely colored.
Love is truly the greatest thing in the world. Nothing
in all the universe can take the place of that passion
of the soul, glowing with human affection. It springs
from the "Kingdom within." It was love that made
the Christ-character unique in history. He, of all
great teachers of the world, was the living incarnation
of the purest, sweetest, divinest love. Other great
religious teachers, like Buddha, inspired their followers with the imperishable force and beauty of this
attribute. But the man Jesus, in his life of love,
compassion, pity and sympathy, is the most human
figure of the ages. Love is the essence of *true religion*.
Science is infinitely accurate, but cold; even as
philosophy is subtle and colorless. We find in religion
the source and strength of the noblest sentiments, fired
by love; and sentiment rules the world.

That is the story told by those thousands of letters
that littered the floor of Burbank's study. Take
passages like these, culled from those letters, so spontaneous and appealing: "Give me just one word of
loving hope." "My soul thirsts for some living force
that may lift me out of my trouble." "Is there a God
worth while?" "If you can find time, do drop me a
line and tell me the secret of your peace and happiness." "My four sons are a blessing to my mother-
heart, but they laugh at the churches." "If God is
love, why so much hatred in the ranks of the clergy."
"Ten of us fellows have turned against this make-
believe religion, forced on us at our college." "We cry
for a reasonable faith."

While men and women—young and old—were uttering this cry of human distress, yearning for a message of love, we find some one hundred and eighty religious sects warring over trifles and abusing one another in language of bitterness. Thoughtful minds refuse to accept a belief that lacks the spirit of love. The Religion of Humanity will have for its supreme test love to God, and love to fellow man. As J. Arthur Thomson has said: "This world is not the abode of the strong alone; it is also the home of the loving." Love as the foundation of religion recalls the strong words of the apostle of love in the New Testament, where he submits the same test in the form of a question: "For he that loveth not his brother whom he hath seen, how can he love God whom he hath not seen?"

So far we have given Burbank's views on the great constructive forces on which the New Religion will be built. What will be its attitude toward the many superstitions that have dominated structural religion? In his "Challenge to Thought," Burbank took a bold stand in relation to the ancient belief in evil spirits, saying: "I nominated myself as an 'infidel' as a challenge to thought for those who are asleep. The word is harmless if properly used. Its stigma has been heaped upon it by unthinking people who associate it with the bogie devil and his malicious works. The devil has never concerned me, as I have always used my own conscience, not the dictum of any cult." That story of the devil and his spiritual cohorts has long been relegated to the place in history allotted to Æsop's fables. Structural religion has used Satan and his host, like the banshees of Celtic creation, as so many instruments of mental torture. However, it serves a useful purpose in revealing the insidious ways in which gross superstitions retain their foothold. Satan is the bugaboo of a false dogmatism long since exploded, but retained in religious systems as an instrument of fear. Jewish religious thought, in its primitive phase, influenced by the Persian, gave it a place in the dualistic system, representing the Kingdom of God in antagonism with the kingdom of the devil. Upon this mythical misconception the theory of redemption was constructed. No man of average intelligence in this age of enlightenment is deluded by such absurd myths. Satan and his host of evil spirits are rejected by modern Judaism as played-out actors in life's drama. Modernists of the Christian faith are no less positive in their attitude.

The insistence on the part of the literalists in Bible exposition upon the existence of a personal devil has done much to lead thoughtful people to turn a deaf ear to the appeals of structural religion. The Bible, he was convinced, must be read, as we read all other books, in the light of our judgment and reason. In this way only may we account for the stories of Satan and his host of evil spirits. The writers of the four Gospels have portrayed their Master in the accepted superstitions of their day. Thus may we account for the story of the "demoniac possessions," the temptation by the devil in the wilderness, the story of the Gadarene swine and numerous other myths evolved from beliefs in magic and witchcraft. When we remember that in the seventeenth century "the majority of educated men still believed in witch-

craft," as Mr. Buckle states, and that at the close of
that century "it flourished with fearful vigor in Massachusetts," as affirmed by Lecky, the historian, we may
well understand that ignorance and superstition
abounded in the beginning of the Christian era. In
the light of science, even as we have rejected the
absurd belief in witchcraft, we are forced to reject
those stories as related in the New Testament.   If
Jesus or any other of the world's older religious teachers lived in our day, Satan could have no place in their
teaching.

There are millions of souls in our land, outside the
pale of any church, who cannot be persuaded to worship a God whose attributes of infinite love and mercy
are proclaimed in the same breath with the doctrine
of eternal torment.   Since the days of Jonathan
Edwards and Charles Spurgeon, who preached a brim-
stone hell of eternal punishment, a great change has
been in process in the attitude of the churches.   That
change has found one of its ablest champions in the
late Dean Farrar, of London, in his writings on
"Eternal Hope."   In Burbank's address in San
Francisco, his language left no doubt as to his personal
belief. Here are his words: "The idea that a good
God would send people to a burning hell is utterly
damnable to me. The ravings of insanity! Superstition gone to seed! I don't want to have anything to
do with such a God." Structural religion has been
trying to explain this accursed superstition and make
it harmonize with a God of love. Its direct consequences, altogether apart from the religious life, have
been disastrous. In the words of Lecky, he believed

that "The doctrine of a material hell in its effect was
to chill and deaden the sympathies, predispose men
to inflict suffering, and to retard the march of civilization." How can the leaders of a religion, he asked,
denounce wars on the ground of cruelty when the faith
they proclaim assigns to eternal perdition innocent
children conceived and born in sin, because the sprink-
ling of water on their persons has been neglected?
How could such a God reign and be at home in heaven,
conscious of the billions of souls crying in vain for a
drop of water to relieve their terrible tortures? No!
the penalty for wrong-doing is now and within us.
The Religion of Humanity will proclaim a hell here
and now, "not in future flames of sulphur in some
far-off prison." This position is endorsed by the mod-
ernist leaders of institutional Christianity. On the
other hand, those who are ardent believers in a material hell refer to the teachings of Jesus as the source
of their conviction.

The opposite position, however, is the only logical
conclusion to draw from the teachings of Jesus, which,
rightfully treated, Burbank thought, admit only of a
spiritual interpretation. It was this same material
conception that led to his rejection and crucifixion. It
is the material interpretation that crucifies him afresh.
No great teacher of a world religion laid greater stress
on the present, and less stress on the future life. His
life and teaching enriched the idea of the abundant
life, as lived here and now. Poets like Milton and
Dante have created by their imagination a heaven and
a hell, in relation to which Jesus was absolutely silent.
His message emphasized God's love, expressed in terms

of truth. Institutional Christianity, as the advocate
of eternal torment, magnifies God's justice, in terms
of falsehood. No reasonable mind would care to enter
into communion with a Being who condemned the
mass of mankind to endless perdition and pain. Whatever power an institutional system may have attained
by insisting on such a state, and by claiming the power
of deliverance therefrom, has been won at an awful
cost. Millions of people agree that it belongs to the
ravings of insanity.

The philosophy of life as interpreted by Jesus,
Burbank proclaimed, is utterly opposed to this horrible doctrine. Reading the story of his ministry, no
reasonable mind can accept any saying, alleged to
have been uttered by him, that is not in perfect
harmony with the weight of his message in revealing the infinite love and compassion of Almighty
God.

Some of his correspondents were interested to learn
what stand the Religion of Humanity will take in relation to the doctrine of expiatory sacrifice. Burbank's
answer was that no such doctrine belongs to a religion
that will proclaim a God of infinite love. It is unworthy our idea of the Creative Being, revealed
through our savior, science. In all primitive religions
craven fear was the inspiring spirit of sacrificial acts,
either propitiatory or expiatory. The lower the social
caste, the more horrible was the nature of the sacrifice.
It passed from older forms into the Hebrew conception of religion. This false and unworthy conception
has maintained a foothold in many forms of modern
structural Christianity. God is looked upon as a stern

judge, demanding the payment of penalty for sin
committed or yet to be committed. This payment is
made by faith in the vicarious shedding of blood, which
remits the penalty and stays the avenging hand. The
ransomed sinner suddenly experiences a conversion,
and is given the assurance of a future paradise, as he
turns from his satiated sensuality or depleted selfish
living. Such a doctrine is an appeal to the individual,
based on his personal safety or welfare. It is sub-
versive of the whole idea of character and rectitude,
rationally considered.

The Religion of Humanity, he believed, will reject
such a scheme of salvation and substitute therefor a
salvation based on self-reformation and self-sacrifice
in the beauty and nobleness of service to fellow man.
A God of infinite love calls for no higher atonement
than that of a life attuned to Him by love and personal
devotion. Thousands of letters received from all parts
of the world in response to his "Challenge to Thought"
were heartily in accord with this rational interpretation of religious belief.

On the subject of belief in miracles as recorded, for
example, in the New Testament, Burbank's idea was
that faith in miracles found a congenial soil in the
gross superstitions of an age in which magic and witchcraft, diabolical possessions and diabolical diseases
were universally accepted as fact. In this age of advanced science, such claims form one of the great
stumbling blocks to the reasonable acceptance of the
Christian faith. They belonged to an age that referred
every problem to the realm of the supernatural. We
live in an age in which the natural is dominant. The

historian, William Lecky, in his *Rationalism in Europe,*
states what he had in mind, he said, with remarkable
accuracy. Thus he writes:

> When it began, Christianity was regarded as a
> system entirely beyond the range and scope of
> human reason: it was impious to question; it was
> impious to examine; it was impious to discrim-
> inate. On the other hand, it was visibly instinct
> with the supernatural. Miracles of every order
> and degree of magnitude were flashing forth in-
> cessantly from all its parts. They excited no
> scepticism and no surprise. The miraculous ele-
> ment pervaded all literature, explained all diffi-
> culties, consecrated all doctrines. Every unusual
> phenomenon was immediately referred to a super-
> natural agency, not because there was a passion
> for the improbable, but because such an explana-
> tion seemed far more simple and easy of belief
> than the obscure theories of science. In the pres-
> ent day Christianity is regarded as a system which
> courts the strictest investigation, and which,
> among many other functions, was designed to
> vivify and stimulate all the energies of man. The
> idea of the miraculous, which a superficial ob-
> server might have deemed its most prominent
> characteristic, has been driven from almost all
> its entrenchments, and now quivers faintly and
> feebly through the mists of eighteen hundred
> years.

In this age of miracles performed by science in
conformity with the laws of Nature, there is no room

for credence in the story of alleged miracles performed by magic in an age of dark superstition.

The Religion of Humanity will be a natural religion. It will be a positive, spiritual power to humanity. It will draw within its fold vast numbers of intelligent minds that have been forced to reject the teachings, steeped in superstition, of all structural religion. It will be a unifying force. The weakness of existing systems of institutional Christianity lies in the unhappy divisions, the bitter dissensions that stultify and destroy.

The New Religion will offer a common ground for all earnest seekers after truth who demand a reasonable interpretation of its mission and office, based on the discoveries of science. There will be a new sense of personal freedom, begotten of accepted truth, untainted by an arrogant dogmatism. It will be hailed with joy by the millions of young minds who are to-day uninfluenced by institutional religion.

For fifty years and over this was the foundation of Burbank's philosophy of life. During all those years, his faith in the infinite, everlasting, almighty God never failed him. He was his closest friend in the loneliness of his life-work, amid the silence of Nature. Often must he have worked amongst his plants till darkness intervened, knowing something of the feelings of the astronomer who gave expression to his experience in the words: "In the deep and silent night everything moves driven by the breath of God." The Religion of Humanity will draw mankind into the beauty and conscious strength of His infinite presence.

IMMORTALITY

In no phase of his religious belief is Luther Burbank less understood and more inaccurately reported than that pertaining to the subject of personal immortality. His persistent silence in the midst of the angry controversy resulting from his public "Challenge to Thought" exaggerated the misunderstanding. It revealed a striking contrast between the man and his critics. While Luther Burbank was laying stress on the power of religious belief in molding human conduct and developing the more abundant life here and now, his critics were chiefly concerned in demanding from him a statement that would throw light on his personal attitude toward belief in a future state. It so happened about that time that a statement by Henry Ford on the doctrine of reincarnation was published by the daily papers, and widely exploited from the pulpits of the land. A reporter, whose spirit of enterprise exceeded his religious knowledge or accuracy of expression, was responsible for an article in which Burbank was made the victim of gross misquotation relative to that doctrine. We were constant companions in those days, and I am in a position to affirm that Burbank had strictly adhered to the unbroken silence that marked his attitude throughout.

Now this negative position on his part was a stand true to type. His Scotch-English ancestry, accentuated by his New England birth and training, helps to explain the habitual reserve that formed a striking trait in his character. He had to be driven into the open. Often he asserted, in my presence, that his right to his personal belief was sacred, and not subject to the blatant challenge of fiery and obtrusive religionists. When they publicly interpreted his silence as conclusive evidence of his "atheistic tendencies," he realized the nature of the influences that were arrayed against him. As a matter of fact, Burbank seldom discussed the subject, and then only in the presence of his closest friends. Thus we find, in his "Challenge to Thought," that the matter of immortality is only briefly referred to in the form of a quotation from the pen of Olive Schreiner.

This silence on the part of Burbank had a deeper source. He did not hesitate to affirm that the subject of immortality occupied a *secondary place* in his religious beliefs. My first prolonged conversation with him on that subject took place during a trip in 1913 through the Northwest and British Columbia, when we were close companions. He was then in his sixty-fourth year, in splendid physical and mental form, and refreshingly wholesome in his outlook upon life. He was delightfully frank with me, expressing his opinions and convictions with freedom, as he discussed the many honest doubts that confronted him in striving to answer that vital question, as old as the book of Job: "If a man die, shall he live again?"

In February and March, 1926, we went over practically the same ground again, and I realized that my companion of 1913 was passing through the same experiences, except that a greater strength of conviction and warmth of feeling had developed during the interval of thirteen years.

One day I recall having read quite slowly to him a striking passage from the "Conclusions" by William James in his *Varieties of Religious Experience,* as follows:

> Religion, in fact, for the great majority of our race *means* Immortality, and nothing else. God is the producer of Immortality; and whoever has doubts of Immortality is written down as an atheist without farther trial. I have said nothing in my lectures [the Gifford Lectures] about Immortality or the beliefs therein, for to me it seems a *secondary point.* If our ideas are only cared for in "Eternity," I do not see why we might not be willing to resign their care to other hands than ours.

The moment I had finished reading, Burbank spoke with a force of conviction that left a deep impression in my life, because he was so unlike the great mass of believers with whom I came in contact in the course of my ministry. He said: "Yes, my dear friend, Professor James has shown remarkable discernment in his position relative to personal immortality, and it is in perfect harmony with both fact and reason. The true goal is missed by the multitude of religionists, because of the abnormal degree of their self-interest. They seem to be blind or indifferent to the fact that our chief concern is life—precious life—here and now. *This* life is the great adventure. It is the immortal present. To love, even as God would have us love; to be true, for truth's sake; to do, for humanity's sake; to suffer, for duty's sake; to live in the ever-conscious sanctity of life, to plunge into its floodtide, inspired and fortified by those ideals, and take the chance boldly and without concern as to the realities of a future heaven or a future hell—that's LIVING! What shall a man give in exchange for such a life!"

I will venture to affirm that no man ever uttered a belief—gave expression to an ideal—with a heart and soul more powerfully attuned to the Infinite Spirit than did Luther Burbank that day. He unconsciously laid bare the secret springs of his life and daily conduct.

Only in the light of the foregoing facts may we hope adequately to appreciate Burbank's intimate sentiments on the subject of immortality that follow. They open out a vision of universal interest. Nor must it be forgotten that they reveal in a very vital sense the basic qualities of the man. Of all men whose religious beliefs have come under my personal study during long years of ministry, no man appealed to me whose attitude toward the subject of personal immortality was marked by a greater desire to eliminate all consideration of self-interest.

With a deep sense of responsibility—as his chosen interpreter—with the supreme desire to pursue his path of thought with unerring accuracy, I will now attempt to give an insight into his sentiments on immortality.

Perhaps no man of modern thought has given the
world such a vivid picture of the conflicting doubts and
yearnings of the soul as the mind dwelt upon death,
and the probabilities of existence after death, as did
Thomas Carlyle. One day, moved by the desire to lead
up to a discussion on the subject of the future life, I
said to Burbank: "Let me read to you a remarkable
record taken from the *Journal* of Thomas Carlyle,
written by him at his home, 24 Cheyne Row, Chelsea,
London, and dated October 14, 1869":

> Three nights ago, stepping out after midnight,
> with my final pipe, and looking up into the stars
> which were clear and numerous, it struck me with
> a strange new kind of feeling, "Hah, in a little
> while I shall have seen you also for the last time.
> God Almighty's own Theatre of Immensity, the
> Infinite made palpable and visible to me; that also
> will be closed, flung-to in my face, and I shall
> never behold that either any more. And I knew
> so little of it: real as was my effort and desire to
> know!" The thought of *this* eternal deprivation
> (even of this, tho' this is such a nothing in com-
> parison!) was sad and painful to me: and then
> a second feeling rose on me, "What is Omnipo-
> tence, that has developed in me these *pieties*,
> these reverences, and infinite affections, should
> actually have said, 'Yes, poor mortals, such of you
> as have gone so far, shall be permitted to go
> farther; hope, despair not.' "

This dramatic soliloquy of Carlyle, written in his seventy-fourth year, as he struggles with the problem of life after death, appeals to me, I added, as an incident of the deepest significance. He, who defined life as a "gleam between two eternities," finds himself overcome by two conflicting feelings as he peers into the future, mastered by the passions both of despair and of hope. "Does not his yearning for the continuance of those nobler qualities of the soul awaken a deep sympathy within you?" I asked.

He replied that Carlyle breathed the spirit of a philosopher as he stood, face to face, before the greatest of all mysteries. He was prepared to go further, and ground his belief on something stronger than sentiment. He thought Emerson was right when he said:

> Here is this wonderful thought [of immortality]. But whence came it? Who put it in the mind? It was not I, it was not you; it is elemental—belongs to thought and virtue, and whenever we have either, we see the beams of this light. When the Master of the universe has points to carry in his government, he impresses his will in the structure of minds. . . . Wherever man ripens, this audacious belief appears. . . . As soon as thought is exercised, this belief is inevitable; as soon as virtue glows, this belief confirms itself. It is a kind of summary or completion of man. . . . The doctrine is not sentimental, but is grounded in the necessities and forces we possess.

Such a belief is a supreme act based on the reasonableness of God's work, he said. No philosophy, however keen; no science, however accurate, can solve a problem infinitely beyond human experience. All-powerful in the demonstration of facts, science is silent as man seeks from such a source an answer to the question of possible life beyond the grave. We need a surer anchorage than feeling. There was a time in his life when he felt the presence of departed friends and heard their voices speaking to him out of the other world. But that day passed out of his life like a spent wave on the strand.

If the hope of immortality were blotted from the lives of our fellow men, the consciousness of the eternal blank that would ensue would be intolerable. No man of his day in Europe was a more merciless critic of structural religion than the French rationalist, Ernest Renan. Strong are his words on the psychological effect upon the world of a belief in an after life:

> The day in which the belief in an after life shall vanish from the earth will witness a terrific moral and spiritual decadence. Some of us, perhaps, might do without it, provided only that others held it fast. But there is no lever capable of raising an entire people if once they have lost their faith in the immortality of the soul.

Renan, in his judgment, was absolutely justified in making that statement. And this fact makes it all the more important to draw up such a conception of the after life as accords with reason. No religion could hope to win the world that eliminated the doctrine of immortality from its teaching. It will find its true place in the Religion of Humanity. But it will differ in its formulation from the dogmatic superstitions of a theological system that have made a travesty of heaven and an inhuman tragedy of hell. It is not so much a question of continued existence as of the nature of that existence. The grotesque conceptions of life after death so jealously cultivated by the leaders of structural Christianity are responsible for much of the present indifference of the great mass of the people toward the subject of personal immortality.

Referring to the nature of existence after death, the gradual evolution of the belief in life after death from the infancy of religions, he said, is clearly outlined in the history of the Israelites. Up to the period of the Babylonian captivity it is evident that the hereafter had no place in their religious beliefs. During the period of their captivity, however, in which for over two centuries they were in close contact with the Persian religion, they took over from that system belief in one God, a heaven and a hell, the resurrection from the dead and the final day of judgment. Then came the crowning stage as contained in the tenets of the Christian faith. It is a history throughout of faith, and faith alone, placed upon alleged fact, beyond the range of human experience.

I submitted to Burbank my personal belief that the integrity of the Christian religion is based on the alleged fact of the resurrection of Jesus from the dead. Thus Paul, in his letter to the Corinthians, took the bold stand: "If Christ be not risen, then is our preaching vain, and your faith is also vain. Yea, and we are found false witnesses of God;

because we have testified of God that He raised up
Christ: whom He raised not up, if so be that the
dead rise not." We know there are millions of men
and women in the world to-day living lives of conse-
crated service, with love toward God and their fellows,
to whom that belief of Paul is the supreme comfort—
the mainstay of human life and purpose. And those
millions are but a small fraction of the countless millions in the procession of the centuries who have lived
and died with supreme faith in the gospel of the
resurrection. Whatever indifference may have gripped
the world in relation to that belief, men and women
cling to it when they face the great adventure. No
man is so brave that the message of the resurrection
does not fail to make him a little braver. This was
my experience as I ministered to our dying comrades
on French soil in the World War. Who can calculate
the stronger faith and calmer assurance that sustained
the hearts of those millions who heard the message of
their Master: "I am the resurrection, and the life:
he that believeth in me, though he were dead, yet
shall he live; And whosoever liveth and believeth in
me shall never die"!

Burbank replied that this Christian conception of
immortality has put hope and joy in the hearts of
millions through the centuries, and therein we rejoice.
It is one of the many gates, wide open, through which
the souls of men pass into the life immortal. The
omnipresent God, Infinite Spirit behind man's destiny,
has many avenues of approach as hundreds of millions
seek the life after death. And it is here that the
Religion of Humanity will be a living force in the

beliefs of men. It will teach the reality of spiritual being and deny the doctrine of a bodily resurrection. It will proclaim the truth of life after death, quite independent of the story of the risen Jesus. Apart altogether from revelation, belief in immortality will be taught as a sequence of evolution. Burbank shared with Charles Darwin his conception of that life when he said: "Believing as I do that man in the distant future will be a far more perfect creature than he now is, it is an intolerable thought that he and other sentient beings are doomed to complete annihilation after such a long-continued slow process." And he believed that such a perfected creature will belong to the realm of the spiritual. The Religion of Humanity will question the position taken by Paul and others that, "since by man came death, by man came also the resurrection of the dead." There's no reason for bringing Adam into the question of the immortal. To him, the life of Jesus in his earthly ministry means more to the world than the story of his resurrected life. No man ever lived who taught the empire of the spiritual with such supernal force, and demonstrated the truth that man is in eternity, traveling across the face of time, with more conclusiveness. He believed in, and lived by, the reality of the "Eternal Now." The Religion of Humanity will take from the page of revelation only such statements on the doctrine of immortality as may harmonize with modern scholarship and the truth of science. "Out of death comes the view of the life beyond the grave. . . . Though death be repugnant to the flesh, just where the Spirit is given, to die is gain. . . . What a wonderful transition it is!" With this sentiment, thus expressed by that great scientist, Michael Faraday, he was in perfect accord.

IMMORTALITY AND REINCARNATION

In the long procession of distinguished scientists and scholars from all parts of the world who traveled the well-worn path to the door of Luther Burbank's cottage were many Hindu leaders and disciples of the Vedanta philosophy of India. So close was the bond between their philosophy of life and that of Burbank that a hospitable welcome always awaited them. His nature quickly responded to their spiritual beliefs, mystical conceptions and the independence that marked their patient methods of research. He felt at home with men in whom serenity of spirit and poise of character were dominant traits. More than one prominent Swami of Vedanta enjoyed the confidence of his friendship, and frequent were the discussions in which the doctrines of reincarnation and transmigration were treated from every angle. It may safely be affirmed that the inspiring motive of his desire to master the Vedantic theory of reincarnation had no connection with a yearning after personal immortality. His interest in this phase of religion, as in the case of all other religious beliefs, was pursued in a spirit in which the element of self was entirely eliminated. His chief concern was to obtain, if possible, a reasonable answer to two questions which were thrust in the foreground of his inquiry. He was deeply interested in the claim that reincarnation was based on evolution, and in the sequel to that claim that reincarnation was founded on the law of cause and effect.

This prologue will help to clear the way for an intelligent analysis of the statements that follow.

Once I called Burbank's attention to the fact that his name had recently been linked with that of Henry Ford in a published statement in which their beliefs in the doctrine of reincarnation had been compared. There were such radical differences between the beliefs expressed in the reported interview with him and the opinions so often advanced by him in my presence that I was convinced he had been altogether misinterpreted. He told me that the story of that alleged interview with him, like so many others, had been evolved from the riotous imagination of a young reporter. If the statement of Mr. Ford's belief in the doctrine of reincarnation was as inaccurate as that imputed to him a comparison is impossible. But why compare? Henry Ford had long been his personal friend, and he held in great esteem the stability and sincerity of his character. For his genius, as one of the world's greatest organizers, he had the most profound respect. If it happened that he had been correctly reported, no man can find fault with him because he expressed his personal belief in the doctrine of reincarnation. It is at once his right and his privilege. His own hesitation in affirming a belief in the preëxistence of the soul or in personal immortality was the logical outcome of a life trained to slow methods in the field of science. If his life-work had placed restraint upon his judgment in things mortal, how much more in things immortal! We must never lose sight of the distinction between opinion and conviction, between the yearning and the belief of the soul.

They play upon our lives, even the strongest of us, as
the clouds and sunshine play upon fields of corn.
Often had he seen life portrayed, he professed to me,
as did Walt Whitman in his *Leaves of Grass,* when
he said:

As to you, Life, I reckon you are the leavings of many
    deaths;
No doubt I have died myself ten thousand times before.

Who has not felt, he asked, like Emerson when he
said: "We wake and find ourselves on a stair. There
are stairs below us which we seem to have ascended;
there are stairs above us, many a one, which go upward
and out of sight"?   Nor does one of the greatest of
our scientists hesitate to express a favorable opinion
on the tenableness of the theory of reincarnation, for
it was Darwin himself who said: "None but hasty
thinkers will reject it on the ground of inherent absurd-
ity. Like the doctrine of evolution itself, that of
transmigration has its roots in the world of reality.'
If he were called upon to choose between the theory
of a miraculous resurrection, as contained in the gospe
story, and the doctrine of reincarnation, which has it
roots in the ages long before the founding of Chris
tianity, as a scientist his choice would rest in a doc
trine that included the pre-existence of the soul. H
denied the proposition subscribed to by some the
logians "that the spiritual nature has been superadde
to the animal nature by some extracosmic spiritu
agency." His own position would be based on th
conclusion of that eminent English scientist, J. Arth
Thomson, even though he might find that it put hi

at variance with the evolutionists: "The world is one, not twofold, the spiritual influx is the primal reality, and there is nothing in the end which was not also in the beginning." But his choice rested not between the theory of a miraculous resurrection and the doctrine of reincarnation. His belief in immortality had no place for the continued life of the individual, for personality in his view is absorbed in the

UNIVERSAL LIFE

He believed that the soul is a part of God and that, consciously or unconsciously, it will endure as long as God lasts. In closing his "Challenge to Thought" he gave expression to his faith in the noble language of Olive Schreiner:

> For the little soul that cries aloud for continued personal existence for itself and its beloved, there is no help. For the soul which knows itself no more as a unit, but as a part of the Universal Unity of which the beloved also is a part, which feels within itself the throb of the Universal Life —for that soul there is no death.

Such an inspiring sentiment, he added, is worthy of being carved in bold letters over the door of every temple in which the Religion of Humanity is taught to seekers after truth.

And its meaning has been simplified in poetic form, for George Eliot has most beautifully expressed the idea of immortality which consists in a growing, spreading, deepening love of humankind. An immortality not of the individual, not of the person, but of

the quality; an immortality of being. Our lives are
not separate lives, but organic lives. Society is one;
the race is one; we inherit all that has gone before;
we add our contribution to all that is passing and
comes after; every deed of ours mingles with the great
current of human life; every thought, every purpose
adds its part in making the future what it is to be.
So we live on in the life of the world we inhabit.

He believed that this is the faith of many earnest
souls who live what seem to others dreary and toil-
some lives, but are cheered by the hope that what they
do with all their might, and as well as they can, is
their honest contribution to the future and their immortal career.

Such faith is a rebuke to that sordid craving for an
immortality of gratification of individual desires and
purely selfish aims.

Thus, in that noble utterance of George Eliot, did
he find the deepest yearning of his soul expressed:

Oh may I join the choir invisible
Of those immortal dead who live again
In minds made better by their presence: live
In pulses stirred to generosity,
In deeds of daring rectitude, in scorn
For miserable aims that end with self,
In thoughts sublime that pierce the night like stars,
And with their mild persistence urge man's search to vaster
    issues.

So to live is heaven:
To make undying music in the world,
Breathing a beauteous order that controls
With growing sway the growing life of man.
So we inherit that sweet purity

For which we struggled, failed, and agonized
With widening retrospect that bred despair.

Rebellious flesh that would not be subdued,
A vicious parent shaming still its child
Poor anxious penitence, is quick dissolved;
Its discords, quenched by meeting harmonies,
Die in the large and charitable air.

And all the rarer, better, truer self,
That sobbed religiously in yearning song,
That watched to ease the burden of the world,
Laboriously tracing what must be,
And what may yet be better—saw within
A worthier image for the sanctuary,
And shaped it forth before the multitude
Divinely human, raising worship so
To higher reverence more mixed with love —
That better self shall live till human time
Shall fold its eyelids, and the human sky
Be gathered like a scroll within the tomb
Unread for ever.

This is life to come,
Which martyred men have made more glorious
For us who strive to follow. May I reach
That purest heaven, be to other souls
The cup of strength in some great agony,
Enkindle generous ardor, feed pure love,
Beget the smiles that have no cruelty—
Be the sweet presence of a good diffused,
And in diffusion ever more intense.
So shall I join the choir invisible
Whose music is the gladness of the world.

SUMMARY

Little did I dream on that day when our final conversation took place that the spirit of my beloved friend Luther Burbank was so soon to "join the choir invisible." Our theme was "immortality," and the name of George Eliot, as we analyzed her faith and quest of the unseen, was frequently on our lips. Between those two earnest seekers after truth there was a likeness in harmony of thought and honesty of purpose that profoundly impressed me. Her faith found its absolute response in him, having its source in what both loved to call the "Kingdom within." Love and fruitage formed the final test, and the supreme desire was to lose one's soul in the good of others. He could well say with her:

> So to live is heaven:
> To make undying music in the world,
> Breathing a beauteous order that controls
> With growing sway the growing life of man.

For some days before he was stricken there were signs of a growing weariness—a desire for rest unusual to him. It was most apparent after he had made himself familiar with the great mass of letters received by him from all parts of the world. For a time he had been buoyed up by the excitement, but now a reaction had set in, indicating extreme exhaustion. The fact was, his sensitive soul received great shocks in this

course of studying with the utmost care letters conceived in narrow bigotry or rife with human distress.
The silent messenger was even then on his way from
the other shore to bear his spirit thence.

Shortly before the dawn of Sunday morn, April 11,
his spirit passed on, and for him the riddle of the universe was solved.

Luther Burbank seemed to have reached the acme of
his powers in the months that immediately preceded
the unfortunate exploitation of his religious beliefs.
In the late autumn of 1925 we were together when a
letter arrived from Mr. Edison, full of exultant joy in
his conscious capacity for almost unlimited work. It
seemed to delight Luther Burbank to the soul, and he
read it aloud with an expression of glee. That afternoon he rolled over on his lawn, rising to his feet with
lightning speed, as if to demonstrate his own agility
as well as exuberance. Few men of his years could
then have matched his physical, mental and spiritual
powers. His untiring energy for one rather frail of
body was remarkable. Life appealed to him as one
long glorious Spring. His mind was planning to
mature his greatest creations in plant life in the period
that would mark the completion of his four score
years. His face was radiant with the joy that over-
flowed his spiritual being during our many talks together those days on the religious life. It seemed to
me as if his spirit echoed the voice of old: "If I take
the wings of the morning, and dwell in the uttermost
parts of the sea, even there shall thy hand lead me, and
thy right hand hold me."

If I were asked to name his one outstanding quality, in my judgment, as the result of long and deep friendship, I should answer that it revealed itself in his one supreme desire to preserve the integrity both of mind and conscience. He was the honestest thinker with whom I ever rubbed minds. His habit of accurate thought in the realm of science was brought into active play in the realm of spirit. This explains his matter-of-fact revolt against superstitious dogmatism, his absolute indifference to popular opinion, his eagerness to welcome newly discovered truth even at the cost of cherished beliefs.

If I were asked to name a quality that was a close second I should answer his emotional health, strong and abiding. That quality, which enabled him to triumph over fatigue and depression, softened his judgments and imparted a beautiful tenderness to his spirit that left its mark in kind upon all who came within the radius of his personality. He had a heart that went out in great love to all humanity. This permanent inward glow helps to account for that almost hypnotic influence felt in his presence by those who were honored with his friendship. These qualities of mind and heart in harmonious combination form the cornerstone of the structure of his character and beliefs.

Luther Burbank perceived in all men the unborn possibilities of the good life, even though surface indications reported them to be as hard as flint or as unresponsive as stone. So great was his spirit of compassion that, in the days of his greatest strength, many a soul sought his help, and moral and physical wrecks regained their grip through his healing power.

To him life—the more abundant life—was ever supreme. He sought that life by fifty years of patient care for the plant of the field and the human plant that he called himself and felt to be molded by the same almighty Force. It can be readily understood that a man of such mold of mind and heart fretted at doctrinal definitions. Theological terms encasing dead beliefs suggested to his mind the decayed wrappings that bind the bodies of Egyptian mummies. Yet there was a sweet reasonableness about his attitude. He was peculiarly free from the too frequent error of modernists who, in assailing the dogmatism of fundamentalists, are not one whit less dogmatic themselves. "What is there to be said on the other side?" was a favorite expression of his, indicating an open mind.

Luther Burbank was at heart a poet, one of Nature's best, for his soul was steeped in the beautiful even though he lacked facility in the power of poetic expression. He was an idealist, with a warmth of passion for his fellow man that flowered in acts of love and fellowship. It is told of St. Francis of Assisi by his biographer, Ozanam, that

> He loved rocks and forests and harvests, the beauty of the fields, the freshness of fountains, the verdant gardens, the earth, the fire, the sea and winds and spoke to them as living creatures, exhorting them to remain pure, and to honor and serve God. The birds and beasts and flowers he spoke of as his brethren and sisters and many sweet stories are told of his compassion to the sufferings of animals—how hunted creatures, the

pheasants and the hares, ran to him for protection, and hid themselves in the folds of his habit.

How near unto this universal love—of nature, of animal life, of mankind—was the saintly Luther Burbank. His were like simple affections, broad and deep as the universe. In the circle of his closest friends where he cast off all reserve, his sayings had all the charm of the spontaneous, in motion, warmth and color. He was most at home in his garden, drinking in the fragrance of dahlias and chrysanthemums, and skipping with joyousness of being like a youth through its narrow trails.

His face was a benediction. There was a delicacy to his features of unusual charm, and his constant smile fascinated all who came into his presence. It was radiant with the glow of the qualities of love, kindness, gentleness and repose. Yet there was an added something to his expression suggesting great force of character—a quickness of decision and action that belong to greatness.

Between his own simple life and the sweet, trustful intuitive life that children lead there was a mutual bond, surpassing beautiful. It was all—everything—taken for granted between them. In his walks, little children would rush toward him with outstretched arms, and pour out the secrets and affections of their hearts, happy and confident in his trustful love.

Religion was the great reality of his being. There did he find the substance, not only of things hoped for, but of things that make beautiful the life that now is. Like many other strong men in the world of science, he shrank from the play of words to demonstrate God, His nature and His attributes as vain. Religion was not that at all, but life finite seeking from life infinite its greatest treasures.

His one dream was of a Religion of Humanity that would appeal to the mass of mankind. A religion, that is, in which religious truth in the large would be disentangled from the meshes of superstition and a unity of belief made possible.

And his supreme aim was to express that religion himself in terms of life. His interests centered in life, the larger, richer life. It seems to me the interpretation of Professor Leuba might be accepted as his conception of that life, when he stated:

> God is not known, He is understood, He is used. If He proves himself useful the religious consciousness asks for no more than that. Does God really exist? How does he exist? What is he? are so many irrelevant questions. Not God, but life, more life, a larger, richer, more satisfying life is, in the last analysis, the end of religion. The love of life, at any and every level of development, is the religious impulse.

Speaking out of an experience of more than forty years in the active ministry, and of a wide and intimate acquaintance with men outside of these professional contacts, Luther Burbank impressed me as the purest, gentlest, kindest, most religious soul that ever entered my life.

Truly, the walks we took in spirit in the many weeks spent by me in his home through the rich pastures of religious thought, plucking the sustenance planted by the hand of God by the way, were to me the most fruitful hours ever spent in the realm of the spiritual.

For fifty years and over he worked with Nature as an accomplice. As he said: "What a joy life is when you have made a close working partnership with Nature, helping her to produce for the benefit of mankind new forms, colors and perfumes in flowers which were never known before; fruits in form, size, color and flavor never before seen on this globe, and grains of enormously increased productiveness." The world has generously acknowledged the thoroughness of his success in that work.

For fifty years and over he worked with God in his garden and in the garden of his soul. Out of the communings of his being, the philosophy of his daily life, the fruitage of his religious experience, he now gives expression to his idea of a RELIGION OF HUMANITY. The world will be no less generous in acknowledging the sincerity that gives it inspiration and the possible success that may attend it.

No summary of his life would be complete without a tribute to the marvelous devotion of his wife, Elizabeth Burbank, whose tenderness and love sustained him through years of his struggle and triumph in the pursuit of science.

If Luther Burbank's spirit has passed, by the process of reincarnation, into the souls of his fellows, God must have chosen the noblest of his children for its abode.

If his spirit has been merged in the eternal consciousness of God, it has surely found a fitting resting place.

If, in the language of evangelical faith, he has been called, as the child of God, into the abiding presence of his eternal Father, the radiancy of his personality will find it to be an environment intensely absorbing.

But who can tell?

Were the aggregate of the world's knowledge in the fields of science concentrated in a single mind, that mind would utterly fail if it tried to demonstrate the nature of man's destiny, to cast even a single ray of light on its inscrutable mystery. Science is "human experience tested and set in order." Immortality is as far removed from experience as the finite is from the infinite. The souls of men look in vain to that source, therefore, for an answer to the question: "If a man die, shall he live again?"

Nor is the search any more rewarding to those who seek the answer through philosophy. The Ingersoll Lectures of Harvard University on the subject of immortality are of chief importance in demonstrating the utter failure of all speculative attempts to solve the mystery. As Sir William Osler, an Ingersoll lecturer, confessed:

> On the question before us [immortality], wide and far your hearts will range from those early days when matins and evensong, evensong and matins, sang the larger hope of humanity into your souls. . . . You will wander through all its phases, to come at last, I trust, to the opinion of Cicero, who had rather be mistaken with Plato

than be in the right with those who deny altogether the life after death; and this is my own
confessio fidei.

Thus far, that is the limit to philosophy's advance
through the ages!

In his *Leaves of Grass,* Walt Whitman did not fail
to make his confession, as the echo of naturalism:

O to confront night, storms, hunger, ridicule, accidents,
    rebuffs, as the trees and animals do . . .
Dear Camerado! I confess I have urged you onward with
    me and still urge you, without the least idea what
    is our destination,
Or whether we shall be victorious, or utterly quell'd and
    defeated.

In the last analysis, our only hope rests in the
"supreme act of faith in the reasonableness of God's
work." So Tennyson felt when he sang:

       Strong Son of God, Immortal Love,
       Whom we, that have not seen thy face,
       By faith and faith alone embrace,
       Believing where we cannot prove.

       Thine are those orbs of light and shade;
       Thou madest life in man and brute;
       Thou madest death; and lo, thy foot
       Is on the skull which thou hast made.

       Thou wilt not leave us in the dust:
       Thou madest man, he knows not why;
       He thinks he was not made to die:
       And thou hast made him: Thou art just.

SAYINGS OF LUTHER BURBANK

One day I said to Luther Burbank, "Won't you gather together, dear friend, a number of your terse sayings that I may use them in my book? Many of them have helped me."

He handed me the following:

1. Truth shall make you free, not leave you in the bondage of superstition and fear.

2. In order to excite veneration things must be hoary with age.

3. We are the latest product of those who have passed before.

4. If we cannot think and see clearer than those who lived in medieval times, then even what we call our Christian civilization has been an utter failure.

5. Those who have made and are making history are not chained to the dead past; they are looking forward to the better understanding of the universe and our own place in Nature. Those objects can never be obtained by spending time turning backward to look at our old tracks. We are creatures, not "worms of the dust."

6. Scientists gladly accept any new truth which can be demonstrated by experiment, that is, proved by the very law of the cosmos. Not so with any new conceptions of religion; these are fought by the use of persecution and venom. Many of the current religious

beliefs literally carried into practice would stampede
humanity into the old jungle ideas and habits.

7. Ignorance of the truth is the only (pardonable
sin; it inevitably lands its dupes in fear and superstition mainly because it is too hard to think. It is so
much easier to be a mental parasite, allowing others to
feed us, thus being led astray by designing deceivers
or self-deceivers, who may be as blind to truth as are
their dupes.

8. Christianity itself was a rebellion from the
shackles of the past. The road to human progress
since then is lined with the graves of martyrs. But
the clear, white light of science has extinguished the
fagots of bigotry wherever it has gone. With most
intelligent people the fear of a future hell and the
devil has passed into oblivion; they do not exist for
most of us.

9. In the minds of those who do not indulge in the
luxury of thinking, prejudice, not open-mindedness, is
still dominant.

10. The art of getting things done is mostly a matter of concentration and the rapid elimination of non-
essentials.

11. A dogmatic system is the result of a perverted
moral judgment under which the pursuit of truth is
impossible.

12. The integrity of one's own mind is of infinitely
more value than adherence to any creed or system.

13. We must choose between a dead faith belonging
to the past and a living, growing, ever-advancing science belonging to the future.

14. An honest search for truth gives suppleness for

harmonious adaptation to an ever-changing environment. Orthodoxy is anchylosis—nobody at home; ring up the undertaker for further information.

15. Yes! It is too true all men have not arrived from Monkeydom; they were consigned as freight and will be found sidetracked at some way-station.

16. All human societies, clubs, churches and schools have their life cycles; vibrant youth is their best season of usefulness; then they begin to crystallize into more or less useless forms.

17. The knowledge and ability to perform useful, honest labor of any kind is of infinitely more importance and value than all the so-called culture of the schools.

18. Any form of education which leaves one less able to meet everyday emergencies and occurrences is unbalanced and vicious and will lead any people to destruction.

19. "Knowledge is power," but it requires to be combined with wisdom to become useful.

20. We must learn that any person who will not accept what he knows to be truth, for the very love of truth alone, is very definitely undermining his mental integrity and destroying his moral fiber.

21. We are now standing upon the threshold of new methods and new discoveries which shall give us imperial dominion in days to come.

22. Growth is a vital process—an evolution—a marshaling of vagrant, unorganized forces into definite forms of beauty, harmony and utility.

23. Repetition is the best means of impressing any one point on the human understanding; it is also the

means which we employ to train animals to do what we wish. And by just the same process we impress plant life.

24. Thrice happy is the man whose youthful passions and appetites have not destroyed his ability at fifty to step lightly, think clearly and love truly.

25. Long life waits on those who practice a daily discriminating temperance in all things.

26. Man has by no means reached the ultimate. The fittest has not yet arrived.

27. Growth in its most simple or most marvelously complicated forms is the architect of beauty, the inspiration of poetry, the builder and sustainer of life; for life itself is only growth, an ever-changing movement toward some object or ideal. Wherever life is found, there also is growth in some direction. The end of growth is the beginning of decay. Growth within is health, content and happiness; and growing things stimulate and enhance growth within.

28. Can we hope for normal, healthy, happy children if they are constantly in an ugly environment? Are we not reasonably sure that these unpropitious conditions will almost swamp a well-balanced normal heredity and utterly overthrow and destroy a weak though otherwise good one? We are learning that child life is far more sensitive to impressions of all kinds than we had ever before realized.

29. We are a garrulous people and too often forget or do not know that the heart as well as the head should receive its full share of culture.

30. A well-balanced character should always be the object and aim of all education.

31. A perfect system of education can never be attained, because education is preparing one for the specific environment expected, while conditions change with time and place. There is too much striving to be consistent rather than to be right.

32. Every great man is at heart a poet, and all must listen long to the harmonies of Nature before they can make successful translations from her infinite resources, through their own ideals, into creations of beauty in words, forms, colors or sounds.

33. Religion rejoices in the happiness of others and helps to make them happy.

34. Science has shown us all we know about what we call God. There is no other real knowledge besides —all else is theorizing without a shadow of proof for those who think.

35. The rich blessings of freedom come only to those who seek the truth for truth's sake alone. "The truth shall make you free."

36. "Prove all things; hold fast to that which is good"; and good things are the true things, not the untrue ones.

37. The astronomer, the artist, the chemist, the laborer, the mechanic, the biologist, the electrician and the physicists of every name are exemplifications of earnest, faithful, persistent effort in revealing fragments of its origin and destiny to humanity.

38. Prayer may be elevating if combined with works, and they who labor with their hands or feet have faith and are generally quite sure to receive an immediate and favorable response.

39. Begging is the prerogative of tramps, not of men born, as it is said, to "rule over all the earth."

40. Belittling the life we have here is blasphemy; you can do nothing—be nothing—as long as you blaspheme in this foolish way. Look within, not without, for strength.

41. Thinking and talking and reading of sin, death and the devil will certainly, by the very law of the universe, bring to you your full share of them.

42. Science, which is only another name for truth, now holds religious charlatans, self-deceivers and God-agents in a certain degree of check—agents and employees, I mean, of a mythical, medieval man-made God, anthropomorphic in constitution.

43. Look for and cultivate the good within yourself, your friends and neighbors; in animals, birds, trees, flowers, fields, rivers, mountains; and in stars which are not holes in the firmament but the light of other cosmic worlds.

44. The word "religion" has acquired a very bad name among those who really love truth, justice, charity. It also exhales the musty odor of sanctimony and falsehood.

45. Church sounds and smells are not as pleasing to many as those of the open, sunny fields of flowers.

46. We are all great travelers, even when we stay at home. We all travel around this little globe 24,000 miles every day, or at the rate of 1,000 miles an hour; and around our central giver of light and life in another direction at the same time at a much more fearful speed; and we travel constantly in a third direction

still at one and the same time. We are now 400 miles
at least from the point in space at which I commenced
speaking to you.

47. It does no good to deceive yourself with outside
false promises; look within for light, peace and
strength—and do not, like cowards, call on others for
help.

48. Cold mathematical intellect unaccompanied by
a heart for the philosophic, idealistic, and poetic side
of Nature is like a locomotive well made but of no
practical value because without fire and steam; a good
knowledge of language, history, geography, mathe-
matics, chemistry, botany, astronomy, geology, etc., is
of some importance, but far more so is the knowledge
that all true success in life depends on integrity; the
knowledge that health, peace, happiness, and content
all come with heartily accepting and daily living by
the "Golden Rule"; the knowledge that dollars, though
of great importance and value, do not necessarily make
one wealthy. A loving devotion to truth is an indication of normal physical and mental health. Hypocrisy
and deceit are only forms of debility, mental imbecility
and bodily disease.

49. A fragrant beehive or a plump, healthy hornets'
nest in good running order often becomes an object
lesson of some importance.

50. The fundamental principles of education should
be the subject of earnest scientific investigation, but
this investigation should be broad, including not only
the theatrical, wordy, memorizing, compiling methods,
but all the causes also which tend to produce men and
women with sane, well-balanced characters.

51. The man or the woman who moves the earth, who is the master rather than the victim of fate, has strong feelings well in hand—a vigilant engineer at the throttle.

52. We should learn that it is not necessary to be selfish in order to succeed. If you happen to get a new idea, don't build a barbed wire fence around it and label it yours. By giving your best thoughts freely others will come to you so freely that you will soon never think of fencing them in. Thoughts refuse to climb barbed wire fences to reach anybody.

53. By placing ourselves in harmony and coöperation with the main high potential line of human progress and welfare, we pick up and receive the benefit of strong magnetic induction currents.

54. Straightforward honesty always pays better dividends than zigzag policy. It gives one individuality, self-respect and power to take the initiative, saving all the trouble of constant tacking to catch the popular breeze. Each human being is endowed, like a steamship, with a tremendous power. The fires of life develop a pressure of steam which, when well disciplined, leads to happiness for ourselves and others; when let run wild it may lead only to pain and destruction.

55. Education of rules and words only for polish and public opinion is of the past. The education of the present and future is to guide these human energies of ours through wind and wave straight to the port desired. Education gives no one any new force. It can only discipline Nature's energies in natural and useful directions so that the voyage of life may be

a useful and happy one—so that life may not be blasted or completely cut off before thought and experience have ripened into useful fruit.

56. When the love of truth for truth's sake—this poetic idealism, this intuitive perception, this growth from within—has been awakened and cultivated, thoughts live and are transmitted into endless forms of beauty and utility. We must cultivate a sturdy self-respect; we must break away from the mere petrified word-pictures of others and cultivate the "still small voice" within.

57. This intuitive consciousness, in union with extensive practical knowledge and "horse sense," has always been the motive power residing in those who have for all time left the human race rich with legacies of useful thought, with ripening harvests of freedom and with ever-increasing stores of wisdom and happiness.

EPILOGUE

In view of the sudden death of Luther Burbank, not long after the conversations with his friend recorded in this volume, I am asked to give a brief account of my own personal relations with him.

My knowledge of Burbank goes back more than thirty years. He had then a growing reputation as a plant breeder and lover of flowers and fruits, skilled in the finest of all fine arts, the creation of new forms, beautiful or useful, through the processes of crossing, selection and segregation. Equally conspicuous was his destruction, at the end of a season, of thousands of plants likely to fall short of his expectations. For, while at times the crossing of unlike forms brings out in the progeny the finest qualities of both parents, and of earlier ancestors as well, far more often it fails to do so, because, in the mass, "commonness prevails." By choosing the most promising of seedlings, however, and segregating these—that is, shutting them off from breeding with the mass—their desirable traits may be more or less definitely fixed, and a new variety or race comes into being.

One quality which distinguished Burbank from other plant breeders was that he could forecast almost instinctively the future of even a tiny seedling. Certain features of foliage or growth mark feeble or worthless little plants, or indicate strong ones. Further, in some cases—apples and plums, for example—years may be saved if, instead of waiting for the little plant to mature and show its value, it is grafted on the limb of a grown tree, and thus led to produce fruit in a very short time. Many young shoots, moreover, can thus be tried out on the same tree. Indeed, Burbank once sent me seventy-five kinds of apples produced from seedling grafts tested on a single tree. As no two seedlings are likely to have had exactly the same ancestry, each one develops as a new kind more or less different from the known female or the unknown male from which it sprang. Of all the seventy-five sorts of apple just mentioned, only one had special value— and that of no economic importance, it being sweet and ripening in October.

Burbank's reputation for fine and accurate work attracted the notice of the distinguished botanist of the University of Amsterdam, Dr. Hugo de Vries, who crossed the ocean and the continent about 1904, chiefly (he said) to make Burbank's personal acquaintance and visit his gardens at Santa Rosa and the neighboring village of Sebastopol. After hearing the enthusiastic and sympathetic report of Dr. de Vries, Dr. Vernon Kellogg, my Stanford colleague, and I were much impressed, and together spent some days at Santa Rosa. The results of our observations were published separately in *The Popular Science Monthly* for January, 1905, and October, 1906. These two articles were later (1908) printed together as a book entitled *The Scientific Aspects of Luther Burbank's Work.* Soon afterward the Carnegie Endowment became